CrEAtiVITiES!

Art Activities Across
the Elementary Curriculum

Charles B. Szeglin

Adrienne Kriebel Holtje

CREATIVITIES!

Art Activities Across the Elementary Curriculum

PARKER PUBLISHING COMPANY
West Nyack, New York 10995

Library of Congress Cataloging-in-Publication Data

Szeglin, Charles B.
   Creativities! : art activities across the elementary curriculum / Charles B. Szeglin and Adrienne Kriebel Holtje
     p. cm.
   "step-by-step art projects to spark students' interest and build academic skills in all content areas."
   Includes index.
   ISBN 0-13-189804-3
   1. Art—Study and teaching (Elementary)—United States.
2. Activity programs in education—United States. I. Holtje, Adrienne Kriebel II. Title.
N362.S95 1991
372.5'044—dc20

90-49901
CIP

ISBN 0-13-189804-3

PARKER PUBLISHING COMPANY
BUSINESS & PROFESSIONAL DIVISION
A division of Simon & Schuster
West Nyack, New York 10995

Printed in the United States of America

Much of the thrust and direction of *CREATIVITIES! Art Activities Across the Elementary Curriculum* comes from Charles Szeglin's 29-year association with the Bergenfield New Jersey, Public Schools as an art teacher, and since 1969, as the Director of Art. As with any work of this nature, there are individuals whose creative spirit, inventiveness, dedication, and understanding of young people contributed to the success of an art program. In past years there were staff members Judith Brendel, Joanne Sciarrone, Marsha Cudworth, Mildred Duchacek, George Lutz and the late Phyllis Scourles, a student teacher, who all brought fresh ideas and directions to the Bergenfield system.

It is with the current base elementary staff, however, that most of the credit for this work belongs: Barbara Farina, Charles Bogusat, Richard Zimmerman and Peter Monchino (until his recent promotion). The hard work, professional dedication, and creative energy of these four are the foundation for this work. Without them it would not have been possible. Acknowledgment must also be made to the administration of the public schools in Bergenfield and to the Board of Education whose support and encouragement that permitted us to forge the program that we now have.

This work is dedicated to Herbert Holtje, Florence Kriebel
Christoph and Anya Mari Szeglin,
and all the students, past and present, of the
Bergenfield Public Schools.

Charles B. Szeglin received his A.B. from Rutgers College and his M.S. from New York's Pratt Institute. He is Director of Art for the Bergenfield (New Jersey) Public Schools, where he is responsible for teaching art, developing curriculum and programs, and evaluating staff. Mr. Szeglin has had extensive exhibits and shows of his work, and has written publications for several local museum and historical societies. His article, "Can We Get the Dinosaurs Out of the Cellar?" appeared in *School Arts*.

Adrienne Kriebel Holtje studied fine arts at the National Academy of Design and commercial art at the New York Phoenix School of Design. She has designed and illustrated greeting cards for several major companies including Norcross, Fravessi-Lamont, as well as covers for *New Jersey Bar Association Magazine*. Mrs. Holtje is the co-author, along with Grace A. Mayr, of *Putting on the School Play* (Parker Publishing Company, 1980).

Creativities! Art Activities Across the Elementary Curriculum offers fifty-six projects that will enliven the many subjects you teach—while delighting and educating all your students. From simple scissor-and-paste craft projects to painting and drawing, you are provided with activities for all seasons and all subjects. For example:

- "Summer Songs" helps develop the children's manipulative skills and can be used with language arts and geography studies.
- "Volumes, Part II—Recyclable Materials" includes skills in mathematics, science, nature/environment, and history.
- "Snowy Day" covers the subject areas of science, nature/environment, social studies, history, and geography.
- "Space Travelers" gives your students a study of mathematics, language arts, science, social studies, history, and geography.

Each activity gives you clear, step-by-step instructions, along with illustrations of the various steps and the finished project.

A special feature of *Creativities!* is the "Skills Index," which lists the activities according to curriculum subject area. Also included is a glossary of art terms.

From fine art to pop art, from crafts to illustrations, *Creativities! Art Activities Across the Elementary Curriculum* will help you challenge students to exercise individual creativity and inventiveness within the framework of the subjects you teach. It will help you prepare children for a world where the arts are not just a source of pleasure, but a way of understanding the world around them.

Charles B. Szeglin
Adrienne Kriebel Holtje

analogous colors. Neighboring colors on a color wheel; for example: red, red-orange, orange, yellow-orange, yellow in that sequence; gained by mixing a primary with its adjacent secondary.

color. A phenomenon of light that allows viewers to differentiate between objects and a quality of objects that can be identified by hue, intensity, and lightness.

color wheel. Pigmented colors spread sequentially e.g. red, red orange, orange, etc. around in a circle. Working from primaries the color wheel includes secondaries and analogous families, and beyond.

complementary. Opposite colors on a color wheel and grouped in pairs; for example: red and green, blue and orange, violet and yellow. Mixing them together in varying amounts changes the intensity of each. They are used in dulling a color.

hue. A pure color undiluted and not dulled; for example: a pure primary red.

line. The extension of a mark or point along the picture plane. Line can vary in character, size, length, and style. It can also have a direction and can be fragmented.

picture plane. The area or surface that confines the limits of the drawing. It may be a whole page or just part of it. The choice of the plane depends upon the assignment or the artist. It can be a shape on a small piece of paper, or it might be an entire wall.

point. The initial mark made upon any surface.

primary colors. Red, yellow, and blue—the basic building blocks of pigment color mixing. Contrast these with commercial primaries (turquoise or cyan, magenta, and yellow) used in color separation in the printing business.

secondary colors. Violet (purple), green, and orange; gained when mixing together two primaries.

shade. Mixing a pure hue (red) with black. Changing the amount of black changes the value saturation.

shape. When a line comes back upon itself and creates an enclosure. Shape can take on any of three types: (1) a *real* shape is that contour, outline, or silhouette of a recognizable object such as an eye, a tomato, a boat; (2) a *geometric* shape is the same as those encountered in math, such as a square, a rectangle, a triangle, a circle; (3) a *free-form* shape is non-objective or something that does not possess a recognizable outline. All shapes are two-dimensional even though they may represent three-dimensional objects.

tempera paint. A waterbased paint made with a pigment, clay filler, and a glue binder. Better quality paints have more pigment and a gum binder. It dries opaque and flat. Also called poster paint.

tertiary colors. Purple-green, orange-green, orange-purple; gained when mixing together two secondaries.

texture. The feel of a surface; the sensation one gets when a hand or finger touches something. Real texture is a rendering of an actual surface achieved by taking a rubbing. Simulated texture is that achieved by mimicking a real surface, using a pencil and undertaking crosshatching, stippling, smudging, etc., to gain desired results.

tint. Mixing a pure hue (red) with white. Changing the amount of white changes the value saturation of the colored tint.

tone. Mixing a pure hue (red) with both black and white.

value. The light and/or dark of a surface. Value is best seen as a scale or angle of lights and darks and grays. In drawing, it is achieved by cross-hatching, using overlays of lines (parallel) placed on top of another until the desired darkness is achieved.

watercolor paint. A waterbased paint made with a pigment and (usually) gum arabic. Better quality paints have better pigments and pure gum binders. It can be thinned with water to bring out its transparent quality. It can be used as a glaze.

Other definitions are found throughout the text.

Subject Area	*Art Activities by Number*
Manipulative Skills	1, 4, 5, 7, 12, 13, 14, 15, 16, 19, 20, 21, 22, 23, 25, 26, 27, 28, 34, 36, 37, 38, 40, 41, 42, 43, 44, 45, 46, 47, 48, 49, 52, 54
Mathematics	1, 4, 8, 10, 11, 12, 13, 14, 25, 27, 28, 29, 30, 42, 43, 44, 45, 46, 47, 48, 49
Language Arts	2, 3, 12, 14, 26, 29, 30, 32, 33, 34, 37, 38, 39, 40, 42, 43, 44, 45, 47, 52, 56
Science	1, 4, 13, 15, 16, 18, 19, 20, 27, 28, 34, 35, 37, 39, 40, 41, 42, 43, 44, 47, 53
Nature/Environment	13, 15, 16, 17, 18, 19, 20, 27, 34, 35, 37, 39, 40, 41, 42, 43, 44, 45, 49, 53
Social Studies	2, 9, 13, 14, 20, 26, 33, 34, 35, 37, 44, 45, 47, 55
History	2, 9, 13, 22, 24, 25, 26, 29, 31, 34, 35, 36, 38, 39, 42, 44, 45, 47, 50, 55
Geography	3, 9, 14, 20, 26, 29, 34, 35, 40, 41, 43, 44, 45, 47, 55, 56

A pencil is an essential tool of communication. This simple yet important tool needs attention in order to produce good results. Start the school year with the students knowing good pencil-managing habits that will enable them to write and draw with ease.

OBJECTIVES

Art
- Learn to manipulate pencils.
- Develop pencil line and value use in imaginative ways.
- Learn to appreciate monochromatic work.

Science
- Learn pencil rendering of natural objects.

Math
- Introduce geometric forms.

MATERIALS NEEDED

- H-2B Venus® drawing pencils
- Smooth 5½″ × 8½″ surface pad
- Pencil sharpeners
- Rulers (optional)
- Erasers

PREPARATION

Obtain pads, hard to soft pencils, and erasers for students to keep individually. Collect visuals of pencil renderings by Jean August Ingres, Henri Matisse, and Picasso.

DIRECTIONS

1. Distribute the materials. There is no need to cover the desks.
2. Ask the students to hold up their pencils. Tell them to be good pals to the pencils. Being a good pal to a pencil means keeping that pencil point sharp. Now it is time for the students to sharpen the pencils with individual sharpeners or the classroom sharpener. The pencil will now be a good pal to the students and help them write legibly and draw more competently. Remind the students that when their pencils become too small to manage well, they should ask for new ones.

3. Talk about holding the pencil. Demonstrate how to hold it in a relaxed manner (for both right-handed students and left-handed students). Caution the students that using a tight grip hinders good writing or drawing. Demonstrate the difference in results with a tight grip and a relaxed hold.

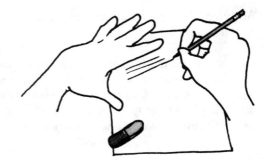

4. Ask the class to try using the pencils, getting the feel of managing the pencil length and the hardness or softness of the lead by using different pressures.

5. As the class is working, tell the students that this lesson is a warm-up for their pad-and-pencil doodle sketchbook. All artists keep a similar pad handy for quick sketches, ideas, and doodles. The pad will be kept by the students to draw on whenever they want. It will be fun to express all sorts of ideas. This is an exercise that is personal and won't have teacher or fellow student input unless asked for.

6. Students can take the pencils and start drawing straight lines, either freehand or with a ruler. They may want to draw computer-style numbers, geometric shapes in an imaginative composition, invent mazes, zigzags, spider webs, and architectural shapes. Suggest using short and long lines, crossing them (crosshatching), and dots. Lines can also be of varying degrees of dark and light.

7. From straight lines, progress to curved lines. Tell the students to just let the pencil glide over the paper surface, leaving a trail of relaxed curves and loops. These can be worked on with lighter and darker areas that give the impression of overlap, shadow side, and dimension. Let the students render what they feel would please them—nonobjective or realistic.

8. Shading can be achieved by holding the pencil on its side and skimming it over the paper surface with varying degrees of pressure to produce light or dark markings.

9. When using a ruler, hold the hand as shown in the illustration. Hold the pencil close to the ruler and guide the motion with the pinky finger.

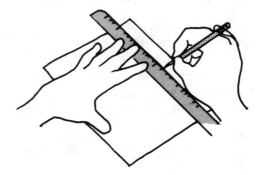

10. When drawing lines, always keep your eye a little ahead of the pencil point. This helps direct your hand to guide the pencil.
11. At this point, let the students do their own experimenting with technique and subject. Remind them throughout the year not to neglect their doodle sketchbook.

FOLLOW-UP

Science

Some students may want to draw studies of natural objects like shells, twigs, stones, and plants used in their studies. Encourage the students to use their doodle pad and leave the objects out for easy access.

Activity 2 ══════════════════════════ I'M BUSY WRITING A BOOK (2-6)

This lively activity is a year-long project involving writing and drawing skills. Using information from their personal history and family experiences, the children will be creating and illustrating a book chapter by chapter. At the end of the school year, the manuscripts and illustrations will be assembled into bound books, ready for showing at a "publication" party. Each book will show writing

and drawing progress throughout the year and will be a record of memories for the student.

OBJECTIVES

Art
- Make an interesting composition.
- Use markers and colored pencils.
- Illustrate written material.

Language Arts
- Learn to interview.
- Take notes.
- Learn report-writing skills.
- Record events.
- Arrange information in sequence.

Social Studies
- Develop understanding of oneself, and one's family and its history.

MATERIALS NEEDED

- Covering for desks
- Envelopes for notes, photos, etc.
- Pencils and erasers
- Rulers
- Pens for final writing
- Colored pencils or markers

- 8½″ × 11″ drawing paper for illustrations
- 8½″ × 11″ lined paper for writing
- Oaktag 8½″ × 11″ two pieces per book

For Making Book Cover
- Colored paper or wallpaper samples
- Heavy cardboard (or chipboard)
- Scissors

- Glue
- Staplers
- Colored tape for spine

PREPARATION:

Allow time each month for the students to work on a new segment of the book. Tell students ahead of time what the theme will be so that information and photos can be collected. If a student has a problem with a particular theme—he or she does not have a pet or there is little information on grandparents—ask the student to suggest another theme. Be as nondirective as possible for the entire project. The same supplies will be used for each activity session.

DIRECTIONS:

1. Introduce the activity by asking the class if anyone knows what a diary is. Is it easy or difficult to remember events? Does anyone know how to conduct an

interview? Tell the class that these skills will help produce a book of their memories by the end of the school year. Explain that each month there will be a new chapter theme to write about and illustrate with drawings and photos. The theme will be announced in plenty of time for all to gather the information for the particular theme. Be sure to show examples of note taking and arranging.

2. SEPTEMBER: The theme is "All About Me." Challenge the students to think about themselves in preparation for drawing a portrait of themselves. These portraits can be just a head-and-shoulders, a profile or a full figure. The students may want to include in the composition objects that mean something to them.

3. Hand out the materials and ask the students to cover their desks.

4. Ask the students to take the plain paper and ruler and rule a ½" border in any color around the paper. The border will enhance the illustration and help the project look like a real book. To save time and have uniformity of pages, you may want to do the same on a copying machine. Ask the students to include many details in their drawing, expressing their individuality. Stress firm coloring, using one color over another and making good use of space.

5. When drawings are complete, ask students to take the lined paper and write about themselves. Challenge them with such questions as, "Who am I?" "What are my likes?" "What don't I like?" "What do I like to do?" "Who are my special friends?" "What do I like about myself?" "What would I like to change about myself?"

6. OCTOBER: This month's theme is a trip taken with one or more family members, a friend, or alone. Select one or two trips that are good subjects to write about and illustrate. The trips might be to a campground, a circus, a carnival, a museum, a pool or lake, a zoo, a show, etc. Writing for this and all other themes should be corrected before the class draws the illustrations. Stress good composition. Tell the class to make the figures fit well in the picture. Make use of the fore-, middle-, and background in the composition.

7. NOVEMBER: Students are charged this month to think about life in their homes. The emphasis will be on living with family members. Ask the class to think about everyday group happenings like eating dinner, playing games, helping around the house, weekend get-togethers, etc. Photos and illustrations can both be used.

8. DECEMBER: This is the month of holidays, so while everyone's in the mood, ask the students to write about any holiday that presents a story to relate and to illustrate. Some of the family holidays that might be chosen are Thanksgiving, Christmas, Chanukah, Easter, Passover, the Fourth of July, Labor Day, Memorial Day, the Chinese New Year, Kwanzaa etc.

9. JANUARY: This month's preparation involves researching family history, with photos if possible. It calls for interviewing grandparents about their family background: family origins, anecdotes, traditions, and stories about special family members. If the grandparents are not near by, information will have to be gathered on tape, by letter, or on video film. This activity will enable the student to get a broader idea of self. Students will need plenty of time to complete this chapter of their book.

10. FEBRUARY: This is the month in which students will be writing about par-

ents. They will demonstrate what they are like, the work they do, their hobbies, special skills, and what they look like. The people they choose to portray may be their parents, step-parents, guardians, or any other care giver. Ask students to think about what family activities center around each grownup; for example, do they go shopping with mom and eat out with dad? The illustrations can include complete figures in portrait style, or show parents involved in work, a sport or a hobby.

11. MARCH: Most families have had a pet at some time. The children will try to recall a special event that revolved around the pet. This activity can have both photos and story illustration. If a student has no pet stories, he or she could write about a pet (real or imaginary) he or she would like to have.

12. APRIL: This is the month that each child will describe a home, city, town, country, or neighborhood environment. It will also include several illustrations, because the subject provides the stimulus for many and varied picture opportunities. In the home are the cooking of meals, brushing of teeth, watching TV, washing the car, etc. Outside the home are parades, playgrounds, historic places, shops, public buildings, concerts, restaurants, etc.

13. MAY: As the book is winding toward completion, the subject the children will be thinking about is school life. The teacher(s), classmates, special events, studies, and sports are some of the subjects the children can write about and illustrate. At the end of this chapter, the students will be thinking of any additional information they would like to add to any of the chapters.

14. JUNE: This is the month to make corrections and additions to the written material. The book must have a title. Photos should be attached to the pages with photo corners or with clear tape barely holding the edges. Write descriptions under the photos. The students are ready to make a table of contents and a title page that can be decorated. Staple the pages together on the left side. There should be a blank oaktag page on top of the pages as well as at the end.

These blank pages will be glued later to the covers and will hold the pages in place.

15. Cut the chipboard cover ahead of time for the students to avoid accidents. The size should be 9″ × 11½″. The cover will be slightly larger than the paper pages.

16. The students will now choose a colored paper or wallpaper for the book cover. Place the paper on a flat surface and place the chipboard on it.

17. Draw lines that extend from the board to the paper's edge.

18. Cut out the corners.

19. Lay the board on the paper. Fold the paper sides over and glue in place.

20. Glue the backs of the front and back blank oaktag sheets to the cardboard.

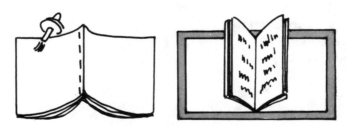

Take colored tape and place it along the left side of the book to create a spine. Take a piece of plain paper for the title and author and cut it to size for placement on the front cover. This can be done in any style the student wishes. The book is now completed!

FOLLOW-UP

Publication Party

Arrange for the school librarian to conduct an authors' party. Invite parents and school officials to give the students reinforcement to continue writing and illustrating in the future. You might do the same with the local public library.

Field Trip to Local Publisher

Plan a field trip to a local publisher. If this is not possible, write to any well-known publisher as most are willing to send helpful information as part of their public relations program.

Cable Television

Local cable television stations welcome local events that they can present. Contact your station about covering the authors' publication party.

Activity **3** ================================== SUMMER SONGS (K-4)

This vacation memory lesson eases everyone into the school year. Summertime means some time away from home. Children take long trips and short trips, across the country, across town. There are big and small adventures to share with others.

OBJECTIVES

Art
- Use crayons, markers or colored pencils.
- Draw a situation from memory.
- Develop self-expression.
- Learn composition.
- Work large.

Language Arts
- Express ideas verbally.
- Think in sequence.
- Develop descriptive word lists.
- Write short essays.

Geography
- Read maps.

MATERIALS

- Covering for desks
- Crayons, markers, or pencils in many colors
- 17″ × 21″ colored backing paper
- 16″ × 20″ newsprint or any fine-grained drawing paper
- Lined paper for writing
- White glue

8

PREPARATION

Collect pictures and photos to inspire the children to recall a vacation or school break event. Plan time for students to verbally comment on their pictures. Try to cover all the students. Lower grades can compile descriptive word lists, others can write short essays. Have maps on hand.

DIRECTIONS

1. Open the lesson with a discussion about events that happened away from home. Talk about a play group or swimming lessons. Talk about means of transportation from walking to the nearest park, or driving to a mall, to an airplane ride to a distant city. Ask students what they saw—different kinds of buildings, landscape changes, different kinds of people, food and amusements. Whether their hike was to a local park or along a forest trail, let them know that each trip is of singular value. Since this is a lesson on making a picture, encourage the recall of one event or special moment that would be easy for a young child to draw. Stress personal experiences.

2. Show prints of paintings, magazine pictures, photos, and former students' work to reinforce the idea of a special journey.

3. Hand out the materials and ask the students to cover the desks or tables.

4. Tell the students to take their black crayon or marker and start drawing their picture-story. Hold up the paper and show them that there is a lot of space to fill, so that working large will help tell the story and make a better looking picture or composition. Remind the students that they are the "star" of the picture.

5. As the children work on their pictures, circulate around the room and ask questions, but refrain from telling them what to do. Young children often forget some aspect of their figures. Stress the full use of space.

6. Ask the students to stop work at the completion of their black outline drawing. Show the students some of the work. Now the coloring operations can begin. They can crayon one color over another if they wish and make broad sweeps for sky and ground. Tell students to add details they may have forgotten.

7. After the work is completed, either you or the students mount it on the colored backing paper with white glue. Put all work on display.

8. Call on the students to discuss their own work; let them tell about both the experiences and what is happening in their own work. Let them locate on a map where the event took place. Try to cover all the students.

Rainbows tell a story, a story of light and color.
Understanding the theory of color through the use of a prism
helps everyone mix and use colors successfully. This activity
introduces color study and its application through the use of
transparent watercolors. These are great warm-up exercises for
watercolor skills.

OBJECTIVES

Art
 • Acquire an art vocabulary.
 • Understand color theory from the color wheel system.
 • Gain skill in handling brushes and a water medium.
 • Learn both wet and dry watercolor techniques (washes, transparencies, stippling, etc.).

Science
 • Discover the effect of light on color.
 • Learn how a prism works through separation of white light.

Math
 • Learn how ratios effect color change.

MATERIALS NEEDED

 • Covering for desks
 • 1″ or ½″ bristle or nylon brush
 • 8″ × 11″ or 11″ × 17″ heavy white drawing paper or water-color paper (three for each lower-grade student; four for each upper-grade student)
 • #4, #7 and #10 watercolor brushes
 • Plastic forks or sticks
 • Paper towels and tissues
 • Round objects for upper grades to use as models

 • Sponge pieces
 • Containers of water
 • Masking tape
 • Pencils and erasers
 • Transparent watercolor sets or tempera paints
 • Plastic coffee can tops for palettes
 • Empty glass jars
 • Prisms
 • 9″ × 12″ or 12″ × 18″ backing paper

PREPARATION

Locate a prism to show spectrum colors. Supply the students with transparent watercolor sets. Have a good supply of glass jars for color demonstrations, and make copies of the color wheel, as well as the art glossary, for each student. Collect plastic coffee can lids to use as palettes. Allow for paint-drying time.

DIRECTIONS

1. Depending on the grade level, introduce the art glossary. Write the list on the chalkboard and hand out copies of the list to each student:
   a. *analogous colors*—neighboring colors on the color wheel
   b. *applicator*—any object used to apply paint
   c. *brush*—implement with hairs or bristles used to apply paint
   d. *to charge*—to fill (charge) the brush with paint
   e. *chromatic*—pertaining to colors
   f. *color wheel*—color-system chart
   g. *complementary colors*—opposites on color wheel; for example, red/green
   h. *cool colors*—receding colors; blue, green, purple
   i. *hue*—a pure color, unadulterated
   j. *opaque*—a dense non-transparent color
   k. *palette*—a surface for mixing colors
   l. *pigments*—paints; coloring matter
   m. *primary colors*—red, yellow, blue
   n. *secondary colors*—orange, green, purple
   o. *shading*—hue plus black
   p. *spectrum*—the bank of primary and secondary colors in sequence
   q. *tertiary colors*—the color between a primary and its neighboring secondary; for example, red orange
   r. *tint*—diluted color or hue plus white
   s. *tone*—hue plus gray
   t. *transparent color*—color that allows underlying color or image to show through
   u. *value*—how light or dark a pigment or painted surface is
   v. *warm colors*—red, yellow, orange
   w. *wash*—a transparent wet pigment application
2. Make a mini-rainbow to show the colors of the spectrum. Take a prism and let the sun shine through it. Color needs light to show color. Ask students to identify the colors as they appear in sequence on the wall. Ask students if they have ever seen a rainbow and if they know what causes it. Upper-grade students can discuss the unseen colors at the end of the spectrum—ultraviolet and infrared. Point out that white sunlight is composed of all colors.
3. Copy the color wheel onto the chalkboard. Hand out the copies of the color wheel to the students. Show and discuss two types of color wheels with traditional primaries (#1) or commercial primaries (#2).

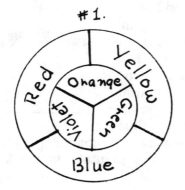
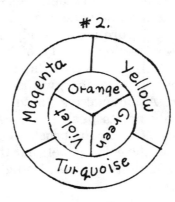

4. Talk briefly about pigments and their use in making us live in a more colorful world. Wall paint, textile dyes, automotive paint, watercolors, oil paints and crayons help us in our creative efforts. Talk about natural and synthetic dyes.

5. Return to the color wheels and explain that these are systems of mixing pigment colors to obtain new colors. Point out how the primary colors (red, yellow and blue or magenta, turquoise and yellow) are mixed to form secondary colors (oranges, greens, violets).

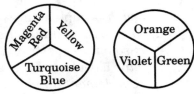

Primary & Secondary colors

6. Distribute materials and have the students cover their desks.

7. Take one of the copies of the color wheel and demonstrate mixing secondary colors.

8. According to grade level, discuss hue, the pure color; saturation, color strength and intensity, and when it is not a pure color.

9. Take the glass jars and ready them for a mixing demonstration. Fill three of them with a very diluted primary (1 teaspoon to one pint of water). Select a student to mix two primaries together in each jar to form secondary colors. Using math ratios (4 yellow to 1 blue for a yellow-green), mix colors that fall in between the primary and the secondary which are analogous colors. Experiment with ratios, because paint brands differ in intensity. Show the difference between traditional and commercial primaries. See color wheel #2.

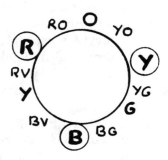

10. Tell students to take their paints and soften the pigments in the watercolor box with a few drops of water in each color (or water down the tempera). Next, charge a brush with yellow and transfer it to the palette. Repeat with a very small amount of blue pigment. Mix together. Colors should range from yellow green to blue green, depending on the amount of blue. Correct, if necessary, by adding more yellow or blue. Add colors to the color wheel.

11. Ask the students to take watercolor paper #1 and apply those mixed colors in lines and shapes on it. Next, have the students mix red and yellow, or magenta and yellow; and red and blue or magenta and turquoise. Apply them on the same paper, leaving plenty of room for more painting. Tell the students to clean their brushes off between charging the brushes with new color. Avoid making "mud." Also caution the students not to push the brushes down on the pigment; rather, the brush should be pulled.

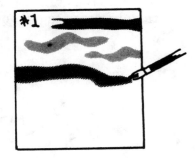

12. Point out on the color wheel that the mixing of complementary (opposite) colors is done to dull the color. Using the diluted paints in jars, ask a student to

dull a bright red by adding a small amount of green. Show the result to the students, and add more green to dull it further. Ask the students to do the same, leaving room for value scale and color mixing on paper exercises.

13. Students will now do a value study, a study of the lightness or darkness of a hue on paper #1. Ask students to take one color and reduce it from its original in-  tensity to a barely visible tint by increasing the amount of water. Dry these value studies overnight.

14. Color mixing on paper means taking a dried color, as prepared on paper #1, and applying another color wash over some of the lines and shapes. The original color will then be a new color. For example, overlaying a wash of blue over a dried yellow will create a green. The transparent blue will permit the yellow to show through. The mixed color occurred on the paper, not on a palette or in a jar. Apply a new wash over various shapes painted on paper #1. When completed, set paper #1 aside for future use.

15. Show the students how various effects are achieved through the use of wet techniques. Take a fresh piece of paper (#2) and dampen the entire paper evenly with a piece of sponge. Remove excess water with a paper towel. Charge a brush with color and gently drop the brush to the surface, and lift it away quickly. Let all students observe how wet color reacts to a wet surface, moving and spreading in surprising ways. Apply a line and a shape. Hold the paper at an angle so that the colors move toward the edge. Blot out several areas of color with a paper towel as the paper dries. The drier the paper, the sharper the shape will appear.

16. Tell the class to take paper #2 and begin experimenting with wet techniques. Students can use their hands as well as brushes and paper towels. Take a stick or a plastic fork and make scratches into the damp paper for a contrasting effect. Discuss the results.

17. Take paper #1 and use it for a dry brush study. Take a *dry* bristle brush and dip it into the pigment. Remove excess paint on a paper towel. Pull the brush across the paper surface. It should have a fur-like effect. A stippled effect is

achieved by holding the brush at a right angle to the paper and moving it up and down in fast, short strokes.

18. Review the students' work. Mount them on the backing paper and put on display. Encourage the students to describe how they achieved the results.
19. Now hand out paper #3, and instruct the students to use all the techniques explored in one imaginative composition.
20. Students in the upper grades will take paper #4 to learn how to give a painted object form. Place a sphere (ball, apple, orange, etc.) near a strong light source. Point out how the range of light to dark defines the solid shape of the object. Note that the cast shadow further exphasizes the form.
21. Before the students begin, demonstrate the color shading used in creating a modeled look of the subject. The base color will be in the light; a complementary color plus some of the base color are used in the shaded areas. The darkest value is near the light side. As you look towards the other edge, you will see the value lighten as it shows reflected light. Ask the students to do two more studies on paper #4, using a wet and then a dry brush technique. Mount on the backing paper and put on display. Keep the work on hand as reference for other projects.

Activity 5 ═══════════════ ELEMENTS OF DESIGN, PART I—POINTS AND LINES (K-2)

Here is a major skills and concept lesson that is applicable to a wide range of art and design activities. The skills of cutting, arranging, and pasting are stressed. This first lesson is the introduction of the first two major design elements: point and line.

OBJECTIVE

Art

+ Relate an art activity to works of art.
+ Introduce basic design elements of point and line.
+ Introduce and explore initial cutting and pasting procedures.
+ Teach students the language of art.
+ Introduce the design principles of arrangement and direction.

MATERIALS NEEDED

- Covering for desks
- Scissors (left- and right-handed)
- Paste, applicators, and rubbing paper
- Envelopes

- 9″ × 12″ black background paper
- 10″ × 13″ backing paper
- Paper scraps of differing sizes and colors
- Chalkboard and chalk

For Class Use
- Selection of hole punchers

PREPARATION

Have a large pair of scissors available, a pile of colored paper scraps, and a paste setup. Collect 20th-century abstract line art for display, as described in step 7 under "Directions."

DIRECTIONS

1. Hand out the materials, and ask the students to cover their desks.
2. Go to a clearly visible chalkboard and place a dot on one of the panels. Ask the students what this dot might be. Answers will include a dot, mark, spot, period, and perhaps even the word desired—point. Tell the class that in art and design, a point is the first thing made. Have the students look around to see if they can find some points in the classroom. Answers might include a tack, a period at the end of a sentence on a chart, a polka dot on someone's shirt or blouse, the pupil of an eye, a freckle, etc.
3. Ask the students how they might be able to make a point. They may answer that it can be done with a crayon, a pencil, a marker, or by wetting a finger and touching the chalkboard. Hold up a pair of scissors and a scrap of paper and ask the students how they might obtain a point by using these materials. Someone will say that you can cut out a point. Show how this can be done by grasping a piece of paper with a thumb and index finger and carefully cutting around the thumb. Trim off the end and you have a point the size of a thumb. Instruct the students to follow the same procedure. Grasp the paper as demonstrated, hold the scissors firmly, and care-

15

fully cut around the thumb. (NOTE: This is the time to check on the grasp and control of the scissors. For some students, it will be the first encounter with such a device. Make sure that both left- and right-handed types are available, although some left-handed youngsters are able to use and prefer right-handed scissors.) Challenge students to make more points, always checking each one to see how the grasp and cutting are progressing. Give help if any are having difficulty. Put aside the points made. If the students are skillful enough, ask them to make other types of points by snipping off segments from a ¼ " × 6" scrap of paper. With cutting skills set, demonstrate how hole punchers can make the job easier. Let students make points with paper punchers. Retain all of these points until later. If the lesson is extended over a period of time, place the points in an envelope.

4. Have the students stop work and give attention to the chalkboard. Return to the first mark (point) made. Tell the students that the point is tired of staying home and wants to go on a trip, so it is going to travel across the board. Take the chalk and extend the point across the surface of the chalkboard. Now ask students what has happened. The responses will vary as before, but someone will say that a line was made. So, *if a point is the first element* of design, then *a line has to be the second* with *the movement of a point across the surface*. Ask the students how they might make a line, and they will reply in a similar manner that it can be done with a pencil, a marker, a wet finger, etc. Now ask them to find some lines within the classroom space. Fluorescent light tubes, the flag pole, chair legs, a broom handle, etc., will be some answers. (NOTE: Before beginning, hold up the scissors, open and close its mouth, and say that it is a very hungry dinosaur, or other animal, that loves to devour paper *but* only if it is fed the right way. The right way is to hold the scissors perpendicular to the paper being cut, with the paper being inserted as far into the open mouth as possible.)

5. Now grasp a piece of paper and a scissors and ask the students how they might make a straight line using these materials. Demonstrate by cutting along the edge of a strip. Challenge them to take a similar strip and see how many straight lines they can cut. Demonstrate to the students what happens when the mouth is not open far enough and when the scissors is not  perpendicular to the paper surface. Show how the paper binds and how control over what is being cut is lessened. Do several example cuts, and let the students follow suit. Circulate among the students and check each one's progress. Reinforce terms, methods, techniques as individual help is given. See which student can cut the most number of straight lines and who can make the thinnest.

6. So far we have talked about points and straight lines. Now we want to introduce other character lines. Ask the students to point out other kinds of lines in the classroom space. The types are virtually endless—the coiled lines of an electrical cord, the bent lines of a bent venetian blind, the curved lines of a chair, the curly lines of hair, the swirled lines of a skirt, the curved lines of

our unfurled flag, the broken lines on a wall chart, the sawtooth mark lines on a box of wax paper, etc. Now that considerable interest has been generated, ask several students to go to the chalkboard to see what kind of lines they can create. Ask seated students how these people are succeeding in making interesting and attractive lines. When complete, ask the chalkboard students to demonstrate how one of the crooked lines can be cut out of paper. Tell them to grasp a sheet of scrap paper and begin to cut an irregular line. Check for proper scissor use and point this out to the class. When the first cut has been made, tell the students that only one-half of the job has been completed and that the other side must be cut exactly the same way.

Demonstrate this. Now challenge the students to cut out a series of their own crooked lines. As examples are completed, stop the work and show them. Keep doing this until every student has had some success in creating a variety of differing crooked lines (wavy, sawtoothed, sharp, smooth, etc.).

7. Check the work from the entire class. The operations listed above may have lasted over several periods. If so, review all phases of the work. Ask students how they might make a broken line. See if they remember how they made the points by snipping segments off a narrow line. By making the segments longer and placing them in a row, we have created a broken line. Challenge the students to do this. Place all completed work in the envelope for safe keeping.

8. Distribute the background paper and the envelope of lines. Set up pasting stations where two to four students share a paste supply, rubbing paper, and applicators. Display a series of 20th-century abstract art in the space, especially examples dealing with lines as subject matter. Prints are ideal for this, particularly the work of Morris Louis, Kenneth Nolan, Jackson Pollock, Mondrian, etc. Draw students' attention to the works of art, and direct discussion to the subject of points and lines. Examine how the individual artists used lines in their work, how they put them down, how they moved them about. Have students empty their envelopes of points and lines onto their paper. Ask them to move the points and lines about on the paper as the master artists did. (Try to keep them thinking in the abstract, regarding the lines as subject matter, as opposed to using them to create objects—another approach to this seminal lesson, which will be handled later.) As the students move the lines and points about, introduce several new terms and ideas: (1) *overlap*—when two lines intersect, with one crossing the other. (2) *direction*—when some lines are vertical, others are horizontal, and still others are diagonal. (3) *arrangement*—the movement and composition of lines and points on a surface.

Encourage diversity and free movement, showing a variety of solutions. Let each student work until he or she is satisfied with the composition.

9. Now the pasting process can begin. Have the class watch as you demonstrate how to paste. (The design can be gently pushed to the side, clearing the surface for work.) Select one line. Take the applicator and apply a very thin coating over the entire length of the piece. (Paste should be transparent.) Invert and place onto the background paper. (Remember not to apply paste to the line while it is on top of the background paper. Use the desk covering for this operation.) Place the rubbing paper on top, apply pressure, remove, and admire the results. To show what *not* to do, purposely add too much paste to another line, invert it, apply rubbing paper, and demonstrate how the paste will be pushed out from the sides. Stress this throughout the lesson. Now ask the students to follow your directions with their first line. Walk about and give individual instructions where needed. Hold up several examples of the first operation and show the rest of the class. Reinforcement always helps. Challenge the students to continue working until all of the points and lines are pasted to the surface of the black paper. As the work is being done, stress and review the terms overlap, arrangement, vertical, horizontal, diagonal. When complete, paste it to colorful backing paper and display. With their work on display, enter into a conversation with the class about the finished products. Reinforce the terms/definitions of the lesson.

FOLLOW-UP

Art

As the year progresses, never fail to use the opportunity to refer to points and lines, as new examples enter the classroom. Encourage students also to bring new and exciting examples to class.

Activity 6 ══════════════════ ELEMENTS OF DESIGN,
PART II—POINTS
AND LINES (K-3)

Here is the second part to the lesson on points and lines. This time, the end product is an objective or subjective creation instead of an abstract one.

OBJECTIVES

Art
- Relate an art activity to works of art.
- Introduce basic design elements of point and line.
- Introduce and explore initial cutting and pasting procedures.
- Teach students the language of art.
- Introduce the design principles of arrangement and direction.
- Creatively assemble a series of basic building blocks into an original idea.
- Develop independent thinking in the assembling of components into a subjective product.

Language Arts
- Write and talk about the development of the project.

MATERIALS NEEDED

See Part I

DIRECTIONS

1. Review steps 1 through 7 from Part I.
2. Distribute the background paper and the envelope of points and lines. Also set up pasting stations where two to four students share a paste supply, rubbing paper, and applicators. Have students empty the contents of the envelopes onto the background paper. Ask the students to gather around one of the desks. Move the pieces around, and ask what might be built with them. Take suggestions from the group, but give some assistance where needed. For example, straight lines can create a box to which two more lines can be added

to form a roof. Once the idea begins to catch on, let the children's imaginations and natural creative impulses take hold. Animals, cars, planes, etc., will emerge.

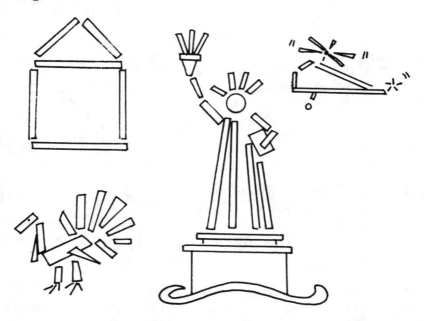

3. Challenge students to create either a single image or as many differing ones as possible. Walk about the classroom as these are being formed by the students. Bring attention to those that are unique, and fill the space in some interesting way, etc.
4. When the final images have been formed, begin the pasting process. (Refer to step 9 in Part I.)

FOLLOW-UP

Language Arts
Students can either write about or talk about their work and the subjects they created.

Activity 7 ━━━━━━━━━ ELEMENTS OF DESIGN, PART III—LINES THAT BEND, BUMP, TURN, AND SPRING (K-3)

Continuing with the lesson on design fundamentals, let's now move from flat lines to those that work into the third dimension. We take our first steps into this world by exploring things that extend from a flat surface in a variety of ways.

OBJECTIVES

Art
- ◆ Distinguish the difference between flat lines and lines in relief.
- ◆ Reinforce the concept of arrangement and composition as it relates to relief.
- ◆ Interrelate abstract art constructions to natural and man-made forms.

Language Arts
- ◆ Use verbal and writing skills to encourage interdisciplinary thinking.

MATERIALS NEEDED

- Covering for desks
- Scissors
- White paste, applicator and rubbing paper
- Pencils
- Backing paper 1″ larger than base paper

- 9″ × 12″ or 10″ × 13″ or 11″ × 14″ construction paper in any color for base paper
- Colored construction paper in various sizes for work paper

PREPARATION

Have a series of large paper strips available for demonstration purposes so that they are better seen by students. Locate photographs of such structures as amusement parks, views of world fairs, Disneyland or Walt Disney World, playgrounds, etc.

DIRECTIONS

1. Review and reinforce Parts I and II that worked with basic design concepts of point and line. Show examples of this work. Ask students to recall the terms, procedures, and concepts that were stressed; for example, point, line, direction, horizontal, vertical, overlap, flatness, etc.
2. Take a piece of paper and ask the students to remember the lesson in which they were challenged to cut a series of straight lines from one piece of paper. Cut several lines and then ask the students to do the same. At this point, review and reinforce cutting techniques introduced earlier. Walk about and provide individual assistance where needed. As usual, point out in a positive manner examples that are being correctly done.
3. Hold up the base paper. Tell the students that they are not to repeat the previous work. Ask how they could attach the lines to the base paper in a new manner. Ask a student to come to the work area if he or she has a solution. If

no solution is given, review the concept of flatness and then introduce the concept of relief—*something that stands out from a flat surface.* Apply paste to one end of a line and paste it to the base paper. Hold up the base paper to demonstrate how the end of the line arches out into space and stands above the flat surface. Paste other end to make arch. Review the term *relief*.

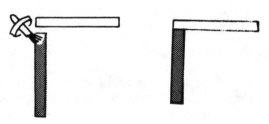

4. Ask students how else one can make lines that stand out from the surface. Answers may include: arch, spiral, spring. Then demonstrate these lines. To make an arch, paste both ends down with the length between held high by placing the ends closer together.

To make a spiral, take a square of paper, cut off each of the points, and round these off to create a circle.

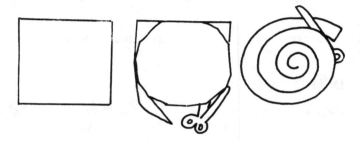

Then cut towards the center by following the outside perimeter (circumference) in a roundabout manner, creating a spiral. The center of this can be pasted down and the spiral pulled out in relief.

To make an interlocking spring, paste two lines together at the ends at a right angle.

Then fold the pasted ends one on top of the other without turning it over.

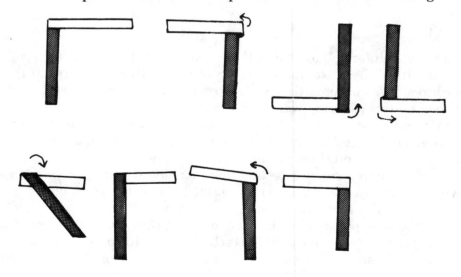

22

When the folding has been completed, paste the remaining open ends together. Release the tension and there is a spring.

When all examples are made, ask the students to suggest uses. For example, a spiral can be pasted at an end and at the center; lines can be cut into 4″ lengths and made into links or loops that can be pasted down.

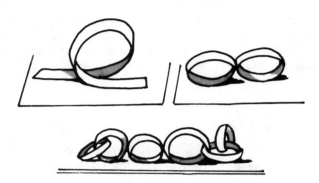

5. After the students have explored a number of relief line variables, refer to available materials, photographs of architectural forms that are in relief from a surface—the arch in St. Louis, Missouri; a roller coaster at an amusement park; the monorail at Walt Disney World; a children's playground with various equipment. Whatever the source, draw the students' attention to the phenomena that exist in the world around us. Challenge them to construct from a given base their own world in relief, their own world of springs, swirls, loops, chains, arches, etc.

6. Let students choose materials as needed. As they work, circulate about the classroom and provide assistance where needed. As in past instances, highlight and make positive comments about those youngsters who are creating interesting compositions. Review and reinforce work on previous lessons I and II where composition and arrangement were stressed. As in past lessons, stress skill development and review cutting techniques.

7. As the work draws to completion and students have arranged their relief designs, draw attention to unusual examples and engage the students in conversation about their work. Have them consider how they might write or talk about these designs. When work is complete, mount with contrasting colored backing and display.

FOLLOW-UP

Art

An alternative approach would be to provide a theme with which to structure the lesson. Rather than encourage each student to seek his or her own solution, present an idea that all can follow as a class.

Language Arts

Use verbal and/or written comments with the display of relief arrangements.

ELEMENTS OF DESIGN, PART IV—GEOMETRIC DESIGNS (3-6)

Working just like the designers of textiles and wallpaper, the students will be arranging and rearranging shapes to arrive at a satisfying design. The project challenges them to make an overall design using rhythmic patterns, spacing, and sequence within a given space.

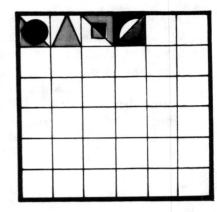

OBJECTIVES

Art

*   Further our understanding of design, especially the principles of repetition, pattern, direction, and balance.
*   Gain an awareness of how art concepts relate to decorative textile and wall-covering designs.
*   Explore color relationships—analogous colors, complementary colors, warm and cool colors, and use them in the design.

History

*   Learn about some aspect of textile design in the United States and Europe.

Math

*   Explore basic geometric shapes, learn how to identify them and how to combine them into composites.

MATERIALS NEEDED

*   Covering for desks
*   Scissors
*   Small pieces of oaktag
*   Pencils and erasers
*   White paste, applicators, and rubbing paper
*   Pail of water and towels
*   6″ paper squares, 3½″ circles, etc., for demonstration
*   Right triangle or 90° corner paper
*   Rulers and compasses
*   Colored paper scraps of about 80-lb weight separated into analogous colors, opposite colors, warm colors, cool colors, etc.
*   Colored background and backing paper of about 80-lb weight, and of a size that depends on the final design size; for example: if 2″ squares are used in the number of 36, then the final size would be 12″ × 12″; if 1″ squares are used, the final size could be the same but you would have 144 squares; the display backing paper would be 14″ × 14″ allowing a 1″ border.

For Teacher

*   Musical tapes and recordings

PREPARATION:

Gather together examples of contemporary art that employs geometric motifs. Gather supporting filmstrips, publications, large-scale prints, etc. Display the prints around the room. If available, display previous student work and/or swatches of fabric or flooring or wallpaper designs that have geometric repeat patterns. Gather examples of Jackson Pollock's and Victor Vasarely's fine art paintings. Precut triangles, circles, and small rectangles for younger students and for demonstration. Use a right triangle to insure right angles.

DIRECTIONS

1. Turn to the students and rapidly clap hands, changing the speed and pitch. STOP. Begin clapping again in a slow modulated manner with the same interval between each clap and with the same volume of clap. STOP. Ask the class to tell the difference. Elicit responses that illustrate components of each clapping exercise—spontaneity and random pattern versus control and predicted pattern. Use any of a number of musical pieces recorded that illustrate this same point. Works of Bach and Beethoven are suggested, but any piece will do. Contrast these with pure undifferentiated sound pieces such as a heavy metal rock phrase or two. See if the students can match clapping to musical pieces. Next, display several prints—Jackson Pollock's lyrical expressionist pieces versus the patterned constructions of Victor Vasarely. Again, ask the students to differentiate between examples. Now, display examples of textiles and/or wallpaper. Select examples from both concepts and again ask the students to differentiate. Tell the students that the purpose of this lesson is to use the second concept—to develop controlled, predictably repetitive patterns in either a simple or complex manner.

2. Draw a large square on the chalkboard. Repeat the clapping exercise again at a slow modulated rate. Ask the students how they could transcribe this to a visual image. Work towards the following: Wet your hand and make a handprint at equal intervals within the square drawn on the board. Make six across and six down for a total of thirty six handprints. Ask the students what this repetition creates, having already given a definition of *repeat* and *repetition*. Look for the word *pattern*. Tell the students that the handprint becomes the building block for the design and is called a *unit*. Have the students find an example of another simple pattern in a textile and/or wallpaper print.

3. Ask the students how they could make this more complex. Alternate a large clap with a small one. Repeat the wet handprints on the chalkboard, alternating yours with those of a student. Try another variation by putting a line through the prints on an alternating basis.

4. Hold up a square of paper. Ask the students how they could repeat the same concept by using the squares. Ask a student to follow through. (Use tacks on a bulletin board or tape on the chalkboard or other convenient surface.) End up with a series of 6″ × 6″ squares set across the board. Review and reinforce the concepts of pattern and repetition. Ask how this same system can be made more complex. Ask one student to add some variety to the repetitive

system by selecting from the collection of precut triangles, circles, and rectangles. For example, students may select a circle and place this at intervals on top of the squares. Ask another student to do any additional move by adding triangles or small rectangles. Whatever is done, the system is always 1-2-1-2-1-2-etc.

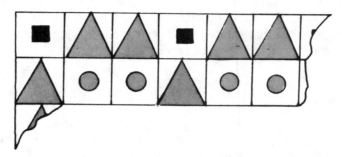

5. Remove the objects from the board and ask students what other ways (using the same series of geometric shapes) they could arrange a controlled and predictable pattern. Look for responses such as 1-2-3, adding a third component to the design or by changing the directions. For example: row one might be all 1-1-1-1-1, and row two might be all 2-2-2-2-2. Then repeat row one.

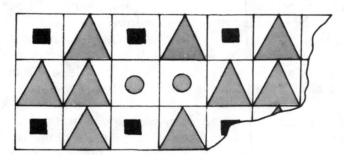

Or the rows might be vertical instead of horizontal. Ask students what this change means. Ask them what horizontal and vertical mean. Elicit responses of direction. Ask the students to find a direction that is neither horizontal nor vertical. Introduce diagonal. Ask a student to create a pattern using a diagonal pattern.

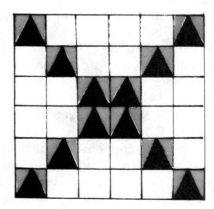 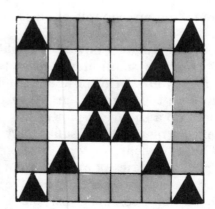

6. Place a single square on the chalkboard. Ask students how they can make this unit more complex. Let them use the prepared triangles, circles, and rectangles or cut out others. Allow several students to undertake the same problem. Leave examples on the board for all to see.

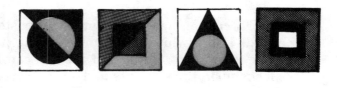

etc.

7. Review color theory from previous lessons. Talk about analogous colors (neighboring colors on a color wheel), warm and cool colors, complementary color (opposites on color wheel), neutral colors (the same family of colors). Select one or more of these as color problems to add to the pattern problem. For example, tell students that they may select two units to be repeated. One must be warm, the other cool. Another problem could be in the red family and the other must be in its complement—green. Or, both units must contain elements from each family. The choices can be endless, depending upon what color problems you wish to have the students tackle. Upper grades can be given more difficult color questions (for example, color themes revolving around complements), while younger students can choose colors they happen to like. Nevertheless, the opportunity exists for a very serious study on color relationships, should you wish to pursue it.

8. Set the rules for the project. Limit the choices, as too many choices create confusion. For example, consider choosing only warm colors or just cool colors. Consider the same family of colors, or colors that are analogous. Limit the direction by asking for all vertical or all horizontal. Limit the units to two; do not use more than three, because the project has so many possibilities and concepts to cover, objectives can easily become lost if too many choices are available.

9. Outline the objectives clearly on the chalkboard. From the scrap pile, let the students select the paper and colors they would like. Stress the working format and size of the geometric unit to be made—1″ or 2″ will fit within the squares. (The large unit is better for younger students.) The making of the geometric shapes can be done in either of two ways. Math skills can be employed to measure and enscribe the squares, circles, triangles, etc., each time they are made. We suggest another method and alternative definition for pattern. Carefully draw images (using the ruler, compass, etc.) onto oaktag. The images can then be cut out and used as patterns or templates for tracing the shapes. You may then cut out as many of the repeated shapes as desired. Uniformity is critical, and the templates help. IMPORTANT: A square is the shape upon which all else is constructed. Therefore, all students must make 2″ or 4″ squares before cutting.

10. When the patterns have been cut out, students can proceed to cut out as many of the same shapes as needed. They might be able to cut two or three at a time. NOTE: Before all of this work is done, ask students to rough out their sequence of shapes so that they can count how many units to make of a selected color.

11. After all cutting has been completed, paste the shapes together in the order desired. Using white paste and rubbing paper, have the students paste together their units; individual designs can number 36, or 144, or even 25. It depends upon the students and your objective.

12. When all work is completed, instruct students to select backing paper and let them rule off a 1″ border. They will arrange their units within this shape. Note that the backing is 1″ greater at each side.

13. Now review and discuss the limits of the project, particularly those that cover the placement of the units onto a surface. Review vertical, horizontal, and diagonal directions; the pattern's spacing or rhythm (1-2-1-2 or 1-2-3-1-2-3 or 1-1-2-2-1-1-2-2, etc.). Challenge students to begin a series of arrangements. As each layout is completed, have the students call you over for a conference. The students should observe each other's work and make mental notes about which one they like best. Have them repeat the process by making another arrangement, and consulting with you again. Ask them to do a third arrangement, so that each student goes through the process of decision-making with pattern limitations several times, understands the process, and will be comfortable with the final layout decision. Having made that decision, the students can paste down the units within the framework of the background paper. Mount on a contrasting color and display.

Activity 9 ══════════════════════════ LOOKING AT PICTURES (K-6)

This activity was designed to meet the goals of Discipline Based Art Education (D.B.A.E.). Although the ideas within D.B.A.E. are not new and much of its focus can be found in the work of many educators, it was not until the Getty Center for Education in the Arts published *Beyond Creating: The Place for Art in America's Schools* that interest increased. This document centered attention on the need for visual arts education programs, because art instruction develops skills necessary for a student's full educational development—and such skills development was found to be lacking in many educational systems across the country.

The aims of a D.B.A.E. program center around four disciplines: (1) art production (studio work), (2) art history, (3) art criticism, and (4) aesthetics. According to Elliot Eisner, "These aims pertain to the four most important activities that one can do with the visual arts: one can create art, understand its place in history and culture, perceive and respond to its qualities, and make reasoned judgments about art and understand the grounds upon which those judgments rest."* "Looking at Pictures" is one way of dealing with these aims.

As an activity, "Looking at Pictures" is important enough to be considered as a separate project *or* it can be used as an integral part of almost every activity in this book. By using concepts and information introduced in the lessons on design (elements and principles) and amplifying this with research about artists and art movements, you

---

*Eisner, Elliot W., "The Role of Discipline Based Art Education in America's Schools," *Art Education,* Vol. 40, No. 5, September 1987, page 15.

can tackle the art history, criticism, and even some of the aesthetics that surround works of art. Students can gain observational and critical awareness skills that can help them better analyze, understand, and gain an appreciation for works of art. The activity has been made as flexible as possible; it is essentially a framework that can be applied to all grade levels and to most activities.

Because the framework must be fleshed out, "Looking at Pictures" requires preliminary work from you. When you have decided on the subject of your lesson, find artists and works of art that best relate to and illustrate the variety of approaches to the subject. This might include prints of artwork, information about the artists (including the period in which they lived—for instance, the social, historical, and economic factors that may have played a part in the artist's time—plus his or her subject matter choices, and techniques of work) and information about the place and meaning of the work in the general stream of art. The amount of information gathered will, of course, depend upon the level of students being taught. More information and research will be required for students in grades 5 and 6 than for those in kindergarten.

OBJECTIVES

Art

- Develop critical assessment skills through the analysis of works of art.
- Identify the basic elements of art (line, shape, value, color, etc.) as they appear in a work of art.
- Identify the basic principles (harmony, balance, direction, etc.) as they are used in works of art.
- Gain an understanding of the final composition and the role played by both the elements and principles.
- Learn about a work of art by analyzing its subject matter.
- Learn how to distinguish between representational and abstract subjects.
- Develop an understanding about the technical aspects of a work and the materials and manner in which they have been employed.

History

- Learn how to refine skills dealing with the historical, social, and economic backgrounds of a work of art.
- See how a work of art mirrors the age in which it was created.

Geography

- Learn about the geographic region in which each artist lived and how the subject matter of the region influenced the artist's work.

Language Arts

- Refine language arts skills through the development of written and/or oral reporting on artists, art movements, and art techniques.

MATERIALS NEEDED

- Films, video programs
- Prints, slides, filmstrips
- Publications, monographs
- Periodicals
- Vocabulary lists of definitions
- Screens
- Television sets
- VCR
- Projectors
- Maps

PREPARATION

Select a series of prints from a group of artists that best represent the objective thrust of the lesson. You must first determine what this is to be. For example, the lesson may dwell on strong observational studies that would best be represented by the works of Rembrandt or Andrew Wyeth, or the approach might be through a more expressive mode, in which the works of Van Gogh or Kirchner would be more appropriate. If abstraction was the objective, then Picasso and Braque might be studied. Whatever the case, you must frame the intent of the lesson beforehand. Any of the above or a mixture of all would be appropriate for use in the self-portrait lesson of the family album. For this lesson we will choose fidelity to the subject, meaning stress will be placed upon strong observational studies. In this example, Rembrandt will be used.

Using either a lecture format in which you have supplied most of the research, or by assigning studies to written projects done individually or by groups of students, prepare materials on the artist and include:

1. Survey of artist's life; the historical period in which he lived; those social, economic, and religious factors that may have affected his life.
2. Survey the artist's work over a period of time; determine its influences; how it changed; how it was regarded by the critics of the period.
3. Survey the mechanical aspects of the artist's work; what were his chosen media; for what purpose were his paintings done (commissioned by religious groups in the church or by individuals); what is most known about his technique today; what sets him apart from others of his period and later.
4. Analysis of the artist's work using design elements and principals (preparation of work seen through point, line shape, value, use of light); analysis of work from a study of the subject matter choices; analysis of work from its emotional impact (what does the painting mean? what effect does it have on the viewer?).
5. Research the place of the artist in the whole field of art (what is his position? rank? was this changed over the years?).
6. Aesthetic response to the artist's work from a viewer with (a) no knowledge of his work, and (b) considerable knowledge of his work.

These areas cover virtually all aspects of the four-part D.B.A.E. scheme, except for the production of individual work. It is best if some knowledge is supplied to students before they begin their studies so that they are better equipped to analyze their own works with respect to those of a master.

DIRECTIONS

Complete either teacher- or student-directed research. Provide the forum (slide lecture, display of prints, video presentations, etc.) for its presentation. Lead students through the three parts of the D.B.A.E. process: art history, criticism, and the aesthetic responses viewers make.

1. Mount a display of prints showing Rembrandt's works. Ask the students to arrange these chronologically to show how the artist perceived himself over the years and how these perceptions changed.

2. Ask the students to review the works with respect to their design components. Is line more important than value and color, or are shapes the major factor in Rembrandt's work?

3. Begin the lesson on self portraits. Distribute the work as outlined under the family album lesson. Provide a mirror for each student. Students should first undertake a series of brief preliminary sketches of themselves before tackling major drawing or painting. Upper grades can handle simple line drawings. Have students make final choices about size, placement of figure on surface, etc., before beginning work. With all pencil work, initial marks should be very light so that many revisions can be made without damaging the paper's surface. When the image has been lightly roughed in, students may then proceed to add texture, details, and value—building up lights and darks, much as Rembrandt did.

4. Throughout the lesson, have students stop work, walk about the space and review their peers' work and look at the examples of Rembrandt's work. Keep doing this until all work is complete. You should make examples of the best student work that is moving towards the observational fidelity illustrated by Rembrandt. This will reinforce the objective of the lesson.

5. When complete, mount the portraits and make a display. Include the works of Rembrandt.

6. Begin again with a presentation and review of the D.B.A.E. process. This time, ask each student to process himself or herself through the stages. Either orally or in writing, have students provide information about: the artist's history and period; influences on the artist's work; major design elements and principles at work in their portraits; and the student's own aesthetic responses to the artist's work.

It is best to use this system in as simple a manner as possible. It becomes very complex when artists from different periods are mixed together. Although it can be done, using single examples works much better.

NOTE: To broaden the D.B.A.E. concept, consider the wealth of projects in this book. When dealing with the unit on abstract design, for example, you can call upon the works of Piet Mondrian as a basis for comparison. Whatever the case, you are the key to making this successful. There are countless programs and sources on the market today that can assist in these endeavors. This illustration is only one example and is not meant to be definitive.

Activity 10 ============ BASIC SHAPES, PART I (K-4)

Now that your students understand points and lines, it is time for them to move on to the rich field of shapes. They can extend their thinking into the two-dimensional world.

OBJECTIVES

Art
- Introduce the concept of shape as a component of line.
- Learn how to identify and differentiate between different types of shapes.
- Identify common geometric shapes.
- Identify as shape the silhouettes of common three-dimensional objects.

Math
- Become acquainted with the mathematical aspects of shape, such as length, width, perimeter, area, etc.

MATERIALS NEEDED

- Covering for desks
- Scissors
- White paste, applicators, and rubbing paper
- Pencils and erasers
- Rulers
- Backing paper 1″ larger than base paper
- 9″ × 12″ or 10″ × 13″ or 11″ × 14″ construction paper in any color for the base paper
- Assorted paper scraps in sizes averaging 4″ × 4″, 4″ × 8″, 3″ × 7″, 2″ × 6″

PREPARATION

Have examples of previous work on lines available for display. Also have a selection of paper scraps and photographs of common objects, as well as several silhouettes of objects, such as a plane, car, or bird. Have some that are not so common, too, such as a curled up cat, a clenched fist, etc., that require more analysis than instant recognition. Have a series of geometric shapes cut out, such as a square, circle, rectangle, etc., for use later. Have some free-form shapes that are nonobjective.

ACTIVITY DIRECTIONS

1. Begin this lesson by reviewing all previous material on points and lines. This is helpful for those who might have forgotten some of the terms and techniques. This material is the important foundation upon which an understanding of shape is built.
2. Have students come to the chalkboard and with chalk review the kinds of lines that one can make. Ask one student to take his or her line on a very exuberant "journey." More than likely, this journey will create a loop or crossover of the line. Stop   the work. Bring the students' attention to this new phenomenon. Ask the students what this new creation is. (NOTE: If the journey does not produce an overlap, then you can initiate it.)
3. Look at the loops and overlaps. Have the students determine the differences between a simple extended line and the enclosure made by overlaps. Ask if anyone in the class can give this new creation a name. The word *shape*

should be forthcoming. When it is, work with the students towards a definition, and use the information for line as a basis. Thus, *when a line moves across a surface, comes back upon itself and forms an enclosure, we have a shape*.

4. Ask other students to come to the chalkboard and see if they can make lines form other shapes.

5. Tell the students that the world around us contains limitless numbers of different kinds of shapes. Tell them that they are now going to play a game to see if they can identify some shapes (or identify some objects by their flat two-dimensional silhouettes). Hold up examples of the more obvious existing shapes. Identification should be relatively easy. Hold up the more complex shapes. When these have been identified, ask the students to see if they can find recognizable shapes in the room environment. Tell the class that this group of shapes can be called real shapes because they are of recognizable objects. They are important for us in making object identifications.

6. Return to the chalkboard and purposely make a nonobjective shape, that is, one having no recognizable form. Ask the class what it is, the answer being that indeed it is a shape but not a real one. Tell the students that this group of shapes is called *free form*. To reinforce the idea again, send several students to the chalkboard and have them design a series of free-form shapes. Ask them if they can find any free-form shapes in the room environment. Answers might include a stain on a windowshade or the floor, a design in a garment, paint spilled on a desk, etc.

7. Now return to the chalkboard and tell the class that there is another group of real shapes that are very important to us that we haven't yet discussed. With a ruler, draw two sides of a square. Draw the third side and see if the students can mentally complete the figure. They will. Ask them if they can remember any other shapes like these and what they are called. Try for the term *geometric*. Ask a class member to go to the chalkboard and draw another geometric shape. Continue until a series has been completed. (With very young students, you might have to hold up the cut-out shapes; however, some in the group will have had the experience and be able to identify them.)

8. Review all of the differing shapes presented. Place a circle on a square. Ask students what has happened. Try to elicit the word *overlap*. Ask the students if this could be done again. Show them a third overlap by placing a smaller square onto the circle.

9. a. Give one student a piece of scrap paper and a pair of scissors. Ask this student to cut out a geometric shape as best as he or she can. Challenge another student to cut out a free-form shape. Challenge a third student to cut out a real shape, such as a leaf, an eye, an apple, etc. While they are working, reinforce their cutting skills. Review all proper procedures and techniques.

   b. Ask students to find geometric shapes in the room environment. Answers will include the rectangular shapes of the side wall, the cover of a book, a piece of paper, etc. Squares might be found in the floor tiles and those in the ceiling. Triangles might be found on flag pedestals and on the alphabet chart. Circles may be found as light fixtures, the tops of trash barrels, characters on maps, etc. Tell the students that these geometric shapes are very important to us.

c. Hold up a piece of rectangular paper. Ask students how they might measure this. Ask them what the long edge is called; the shorter edge. Look for the terms *length* and *width*. With older students, move into the concept of area. Where appropriate from math curriculum, introduce the same for squares, triangles, and circles. Ask the students why it is important to be able to measure geometric shapes. Now return to the school room wall. Tell the students that this will have to be painted. To do this, the wall will have to be measured because the salesperson at the paint store needs to know the area of the wall so that the salesperson can tell us how much paint to buy. Use other examples to show why measurement and concept of length, width, and area are very important and practical for us.

d. Making a circle without a compass can be a difficult task but made easy by following some suggestions. Hand out a square of paper. Have the students place their thumb in the middle of the paper. With scissors, cut off each of the four corners. Then cut off the eight corners just made. Then cut along the points in a line, cutting off all of the remaining points to achieve a pretty good circle without a compass.

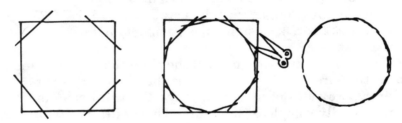

10. CONTEST TIME FOR KINDERGARTEN: Select an easy shape, such as a rectangle. Hand out a large rectangular piece of 5″ × 8″ paper. Ask the students to make one cut to see if they can make a smaller rectangle. Follow this exercise carefully, and walk around the room checking on control and cutting practices. As cutting proceeds and a rectangle is made, ask the students to make several others but of differing sizes. (This lesson is controlled to assist the youngest students with a difficult concept and practice. As skills increase, add other shapes.) In this instance, it is important to assure that all students are on the task and have been monitored through each step.

11. CONTEST TIME FOR GRADES 1-3: Tell the students that you are going to hold a contest to see who can make (1) the most shapes, (2) the most unusual free-form shapes, and (3) the most unusual real shapes, etc. Pass out the paper, scraps, scissors, and pencils (if needed).

12. As shapes are cut out, stop work and hold up examples that are unusual, well cut, have fine geometric qualities, etc. As work progresses, hold up examples that are compound shapes—those in which one shape fits into another. Introduce the concept of variation. Tell the students that shapes can be the same, but they can vary

34

because of color. Ask how else they might vary. Introduce concept of size. Have the students vary the size.

13. Rather than select one contest winner, reward the entire class for their hard work by handing out a nutritious treat or providing some other pleasurable alternative (both at your discretion).

14. After a series of shapes has been cut out, challenge the students to assemble them. Review the design principles mentioned before, such as direction, variation, balance, and harmony, employed with the line projects. *Balance is seen as the weight of objects on a surface.* When a paper is folded in half and equal objects appear on both sides, then the arrangement is said to be balanced. If not, it is said to be imbalanced. *Harmony is seen as something pleasurable to the eye, achieved through the use of similar colors or shapes.* These concepts can be introduced and the others reviewed. Now, stop work. Review the students' progress. Point out successful arrangements and compositions. Let the students see some of the more unusual ones. After this has been done, students can return to their seats to finish their own compositions. Walk about the room giving assistance where needed. After the work is complete, review pasting techniques and procedures, and paste the shapes onto the base paper.

15. a. The final part of this complex lesson on shapes can take any one of several directions. You can choose to use one method with a younger class and another with an older class. The lesson is so important that it can be repeated in each grade K-4. In fact, it has application in every grade through foundation work at an art school. Several solutions are listed here.

   b. NONOBJECTIVE ARRANGEMENT FOR KINDERGARTEN: When all of the varying shapes have been cut out, challenge the students to make an arrangement. What is made is less important than the cutting and pasting skills that are employed. Stress pasting one shape on top of another. Emphasize overlapping and the use of the entire base surface. Hand out base paper, pasting materials, etc. Challenge the students to make the best arrangement possible, without any preconceived notion as to an image.

   c. OBJECTIVE ARRANGEMENT FOR GRADES K-1: When all of the shapes have been made, challenge the students to make an arrangement. Assemble the class around one student's desk. Place several shapes on the desk and begin to suggest an object, such as a car, a plane, a house, etc. Ask the seated student what he or she might be able to assemble. Have the remaining students return to their seats, and challenge them to see what they can make. *(There is no pasting yet.)* Circulate about the room. As interesting arrangements are made, point them out. Have students select the most unusual one and paste it down. Review correct pasting procedures and techniques.

   d. ARRANGEMENT FOR GRADES 1-3: When all shapes have been completed, challenge the students to make one class arrangement. Suggest a total pictorial theme such as a park scene, a zoo, a city street, transportation, etc. Have students at their seats begin to arrange shapes into pictures.

35

FOLLOW-UP

Math

The completed work can be displayed on a math bulletin board showing how simple geometric shapes can be used to create designs or objective pictures.

Language Arts

The pictorial and objective pictures can be used as a base for writing a brief paragraph about the image or illustration.

Geography

Copy the outline shape of your state. Which state shapes are free form? Which are geometric?

Activity 11 ═══════════ BASIC SHAPES, PART II— GEOMETRICS (2-4)

Don't be intimidated by this activity's title! Arranging shapes, tones, and colors to get a pleasing and effective design is a stimulating experience. The mind and the eyes will be busy evaluating each combination—its relationship to itself and the overall design. This is a good tonal lesson to give before weaving lessons begin.

OBJECTIVE

Art

- Learn design principles.
- Pay attention to tonal qualities.
- Increase manipulative, cutting, and pasting skills.

Math

- Learn basic geometric shapes.
- Increase measuring skills.

MATERIALS NEEDED

- Covering for desks
- Colored construction paper in a variety of colors and tones, 2" squares
- 10" × 12" or 12" × 14" or 12" × 12" white or black background paper

- Pencils and erasers
- Rulers
- Scissors
- Paste and applicators
- Compasses
- Rubbing paper

PREPARATION

Collect a wide range of colored construction paper in dark, light, and medi-um tones. Prepare several samples to show the students or use previous student work. To save time, rule 2″ squares on the white or black background paper.

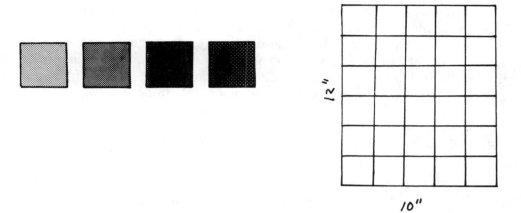

DIRECTIONS

1. Distribute the materials, and ask students to cover their desks.
2. Ask the students to take the colored paper and rule 2″ squares. On some of the squares, draw triangles. On others, draw circles, either with a compass or freehand, and leave other squares blank. To draw a freehand circle, draw lines across the corners and draw a circular shape touching the lines' and squares' sides.

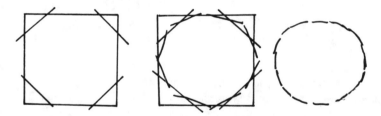

   On the chalkboard, draw a right triangle, an equilateral, an isosceles, and obtuse triangle. See if anyone can pronounce those funny-sounding names. Tell the students to work from those shapes. After the triangles and circles are completed, tell the students to cut them out, saving the scraps for future lessons using negative shapes, Activity 16 and non-objective designs, Activity 50.

3. Direct the students to take their cut-out squares, circles, and triangles and start arranging them in individual combinations. Circles can be placed on squares, triangles on circles, etc. Ask the students to pay attention to color combinations, tonal qualities such as dark on light, middle tones on dark or lighter colors, even middle tone with middle tone. There will be a lot of experimental groupings. When the color, shape, and tonal squares have been arranged, tell the students to paste them, using care so that the paste will not show beyond the shapes. (Review the pasting techniques in Activities 7 and 8.)

37

4. After the squares have been completed, the class will be ready to arrange them on the design background paper. At this point, show your ready-made samples or previous students' work. Explain how the layout was planned. Point out repeats, checkerboard patterns, dark and light groupings, etc.

5. Now the students are ready to arrange and paste their squares in place. Have them decide whether or not to choose a light or dark ruled background paper.

6. As the students work on the designs, move around the area and offer help if needed. When the work is completed, put it on display and ask for a class discussion about this lesson and the previous basic shape lessons.

FOLLOW-UP

Art

Repeat the previous assignment, but instead of using various color combinations, use black, white, and gray for the tonal arrangements.

Math

Depending on the class level, introduce beginning geometry.

Science

Compose an arrangement using the phases of the moon with minimum color and tonal choices.

Activity 12 ================= VOLUMES, PART I— THREE-DIMENSIONAL ART (K-6)

Here is a project that nails down math concepts and will help students unravel the mysteries of volume—three-dimensional forms that occupy space. It can be a spiral project, progressing level by level through grade 6. Opening the door of understanding volume construction will let the students enter with a wonderful parade of imaginative objects made from cylinders, pyramids, cones, boxes, and cubes.

OBJECTIVES:

Art
- Increase visual skills.
- Improve problem-solving skills with size and shape choices.
- Learn careful cutting, pasting, and joining skills.
- Learn to work with flat and dimensional shapes.

Math
- Improve measuring skills.
- Construct simple volumes—cylinder, cone, pyramid.

- Construct complex volumes—parallelepipid, cube.
- Apply math concepts of area and volume.
- Gain a working knowledge of formula and application.

MATERIALS NEEDED

- Covering for desks
- Pencils
- Erasers
- Rulers
- Scissors
- White paste and applicators
- Rubbing paper (clean newsprint)
- Compasses
- Staplers and staples
- Tape
- Scrap paper in various sizes (8″ × 18″, 6″ × 18″) and colors

- Pieces of 80-lb construction paper in the following sizes (numbers may vary if more than one of each volume is made): *cylinders*—12″ × 18″, 9″ × 12″, 6″ × 9″; *pyramids and cones*—12″ × 12″, 9″ × 9″, 8″ × 8″, 6″ × 6″, 4″ × 4″; *parallelepipids*—12″ × 18″, 9″ × 12″; *cubes*—12″ × 17″, 9″ × 13″, 4″ × 4″

PREPARATION

Cut the paper and make several volume models showing different sizes of each volume. Prepare accessories (eyes, notes, hands, etc.) from scrap paper that will be attached to the final form. Plan to use white paste instead of white glue because adhesion is usually stronger. Make several cylinder people for samples. Plan for adequate space for project display. Cut out two-dimensional triangles, squares, rectangles, and circles for class identification.

OVERVIEW

This is meant to be a spiral lesson that begins with making simple forms in grades K-1, reinforces and reviews them in grade 2, and adds new information and problems in grade 3. Review and progress can continue through grade 6. The skills learned are so important that they should be repeated every year, or at least every other year, for example, K, 2, 4, and 6. If repeated every year, the final assemblage can differ by using different colors or working on a seasonal theme such as Halloween, Thanksgiving, Christmas, etc., or by using a topical theme of robots, animals, transportation, architecture, etc. Cognitive and manipulative skills will develop greatly over the span of time.

DIRECTIONS

The Cylinder (grades K-1 and above)

1. Introduce the lesson by holding up a selection of flat two-dimensional geometric shapes showing triangles, squares, rectangles, and circles. Ask the class to identify these. Hold up a rect-

angle and ask the students how this could be measured. Encourage responses regarding length and width. Acquaint older students with terms such as perimeter and area. Taking the rectangle, bring both ends around until they meet. Ask the students what the flat piece of paper has become. Responses will include: tube, pipe, circle, etc. Now introduce the term *cylinder*. Ask the students how a cylinder differs from a rectangle. Direct the responses toward the idea that it takes up space, occupies space, and can be seen from all sides.

2. Hand out the materials and ask the students to cover their desks.

3. Apply white paste to one long end of the rectangle. Form a cylinder by overlapping the pasted end over the opposite end. Apply pressure until the adhesive sets. Set aside. Talk about different kinds of cylinders—fat, thin, long, short. Make fat or thin cylinders by changing the overlap and pasting the longer or shorter sides together. NOTE: Place small hands through cylinder for good adhesion or use a ruler. If adhesion is a problem, use a stapler.

4. After a series of cylinders has been completed, ask the students to point out cylinder forms seen around the school. Look for chair legs, lighting tubes, fixture supports, pipes, crayons, outside flag poles, etc. Continue this line of inquiry and discuss arms, legs, and other cylinder shapes in the world around us. There are water glasses, soda cans, telephone poles, steam pipes, silos, gas storage tanks, tree trunks, tank trucks, and tank cars.

5. When enough interest has been generated, lead the discussion toward suggestions of making objects with different size cylinders. Have students creatively decide what a variety of cylinders can become: a racing car, a tree, a locomotive, or perhaps a dinosaur! Each student will choose a subject and assemble it. (Steps  8 through 12 can help show ways of assembling the various parts of the object.) Another creative method of learning is to choose a particular theme such as *Funny Cylinder People*. Directions for this amusing and basic cylinder project follow.

6. Select a 12″ × 18″ piece of paper and form a large cylinder, as described in step 3. Ask the students how they might take this plain basic shape and use their fun-loving imaginations to add eyes, noses, etc., to make a humorous

character. Ask for suggestions, such as large bubbly eyes, a big wide mouth, big flat feet, any exaggerated feature, or piece of clothing. Following their suggestions, make some "people," using tape instead of paste for a fast demonstration. Keep the "people" on display for class reference.

7. Hand out the materials and ask the students to cover their desks.

8. Ask the students to take a 12″ × 18″ sheet of colored construction paper and imitate you making a cylinder, as described in step 3. After the cylinder has been formed and the paste has set, demonstrate how to close off the top so there is a base for the hair and hat. Take scissors and cut a full scissor length around the top of the cylinder. These cuts should measure about 2½″ deep and be 2″ apart. Bend over the cut segments. They are called *tabs*. Take an 8″ square of paper and place the tab end on it. Trace around the cylinder

to make a circle that will fit over the tab end and enclose it. Cut out the circle, paste the tabs in place, and paste the circle on top of the tabs. This will enclose the end and will be the method for use in other projects.
NOTE: Place hand inside of cylinder for good adhesion.

9. Next, the hair and hat will be made. For hair, take a piece of 8″ × 18″ colored paper and fold it in half. Measure 1″ from the fold and draw a line. Cut ½″- or ¼″-wide lines from the edges to the line near the fold. Open the paper and crush the "hair" for a rumpled effect. For curly hair, roll the ends over a pencil or pull the strips over one edge of a scissors, as if curling ribbon for a gift package. Paste the

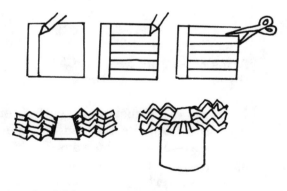

hair on the closed end of the cylinder and add bangs if wanted.

10. To make a hat, take a piece of 8″ × 18″ paper and make a cylinder, smaller than the one that will be the body. Show the students that by making a larger overlap, the cylinder will be smaller. Apply paste, press, and let dry. (Use hands or a ruler if necessary.)
    a. Take scissors and cut tabs on both ends.
    b. Fold one end inward.
    c. To make the top of the hat, place the cylinder on paper and trace and cut as in step 8.

d. After this is done, paste the tabs in place on one end and paste the circle on that end. Take two pieces of 12″ × 12″ construction paper and place the top end of the hat on one in the center. Draw a brim that will be larger than the body of the hat.

e. Cut out the brim and place it on the second piece of paper. Trace the outline and cut it out. This second side will reinforce the brim. Take the top end of the hat, center it, and trace. This circle will now be cut out. Take the first brim and center the hat with tabs spread outward. Paste in place. Fit the cut-out center brim over the cylinder and paste it onto the brim bottom. Paste the hat over the hair.

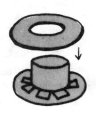

11. Arms can be made from 6″ × 12″ paper. The cylinder arms are then placed through holes cut in the body sides. Hands or mittens can be attached to the open ends.

12. Now we can experiment with humorous possibilities. Eyes can be made that bulge, twinkle, droop, look up, look down, or look sideways. They can be attached with springs (folded paper). These will provide added dimension and interest. Remember to design all the important parts of the eye—the pupil, lid, iris, lashes, and brows— yet maintain individuality.

13. After the eyes are done, have the students turn their attention to making a nose. This can be another small cylinder shape or a flat shape. For a cylinder nose, take a piece of scrap paper, roll it into a cylinder to size, and paste. Cut tabs on one side, bend outward, and paste on the body. Draw and cut out a mouth, with lips and teeth if the funny person is smiling.

14. Now, stop. Review the work by checking on good cutting and pasting procedures. Show innovative examples.

15. Turn students' attention to the task of making ears. These can be flat shapes that resemble ears or simple circles cut out and bent. They can be pasted to the body cylinder and poked through the hair. They can also be small cylinders.

16. Now, make the feet or shoes. These can be big and floppy looking. Draw and cut out, and include a tab at the back of the foot or shoe for attaching to the inside of the cylinder body.

17. Prior to completion, hold up a figure and ask the students to offer suggestions concerning further additions. These additions should include as many cylinder shapes as possible, such as ski poles, magic wands, binoculars, flutes, golf clubs, etc., plus anything else that would make a humorous-looking project.

18. When completed, have the students view all the cylinder people, each one should be different and reflect the individual creative bent of the student artist. Play a game and see who used the most cylinders. Ask the students to pick out the pieces that best show careful cutting, joining, and assembling.

19. Put all work on display and invite other classes to see and enjoy the humor of these funny constructions.

The Pyramid (grades 2 and above)

1. Review the making of a cylinder, stressing again the change of a flat surface into a three-dimensional object. Reviewing and reinforcing the terms and concepts can never be done enough.

2. Hand out the materials (refer to the list of materials for the paper sizes), and ask students to cover their desks.

3. Demonstrate the making of a pyramid, and ask the students to follow along. Take a large square piece of paper. Take two diagonally opposite points and fold the paper in half, creating a triangle. Ask the students to identify the shape. Open it up and make a similar fold from the other two points. Take scissors and cut along one fold to the center *but no further*. Ask the students what this can become. Eventually, someone will form a pyra-

mid. Have the students follow the procedure. Add a thin transparent coat of white paste to one of the cut sides, place a cut side next to the nearest fold and hold in place for good adhesion. This will form a three-sided pyramid.

4. Introduce a discussion on pyramids by suggesting there are pyramid shapes in the classroom. Have the students discover similarities such as the room's corner (the meeting of the walls and ceiling), box corners, tripod stand base. Ask the students about the famous pyramids in Egypt, Mexico and Central America.

5. To increase skills and reinforce information, challenge the students to make a series of different-sized pyramids from the paper squares of varying sizes. Upper-level groups can see who can make the smallest pyramid from a 1″ or ½″ square paper.

6. At this point, either challenge the class to make an assemblage of just pyramids or combine some pyramids with some previously made cylinders. Add flat decorative shapes for interest. A second funny person can be made with the body, hat, nose, etc., of pyramid shapes. This can be called the "Funny Pyramid Person." Stress again the inventive use of materials and skillful cutting, pasting, joining, and assembling.

The Cone (grades 3 and above)

In this section dealing with volume, the learning process involves skill development through the use of pencils and compasses. It can be an entertaining way of introducing skills necessary for mastery of a major math tool.

1. Quickly review cylinder and pyramid construction, emphasizing the three-dimensional aspect.

2. Introduce the students to the compass. If possible, use a large wooden model (which holds a piece of chalk) to demonstrate its use on the chalkboard. Ask students to take turns learning how to manipulate the large compass.

3. Hand out materials and ask students to cover their desks. Provide as many individual metal compasses as possible.

4. Take some scrap paper and demonstrate how to inscribe a circle using a metal compass. Stress the importance of keeping the metal needle point on a fixed central point. For right-handed students, tip the compass to the right-hand side to create an angle as it intersects with the paper. Move the compass, keeping the same angle. Left-handed students should reverse the procedure. This positioning will help in making even-looking circles. Tell students to check that their pencil points are sharp and of equal length with the compass needle point. Instruct them to grip the compass between the thumb and index and ring fingers, and to take scrap paper and begin practicing making circles. Walk around the classroom and give assistance where needed. Following the practice session, hand out 8″ square pieces of paper. Tell the students to take a ruler and find the center by connecting diagonally opposite corners with a lightly drawn pencil line. Where the lines intersect is the cen-

ter. Tell the students to take the compass and place the needle point exactly on the center point and inscribe a circle.

5. Check the results. When satisfied, have the students cut out the circle. Review taking flat shapes and making them three-dimensional. Explain what a radius is. Start demonstrating the making of a cone by cutting the radius from the circle edge to the center point. Have the class follow suit.

6. Now ask the students if anyone can take this flat shape and manipulate it into a cone. After the first success, the rest will soon follow. The radial cut enables the making of a flat surface into a three-dimensional one by overlapping one cut side over another. Demonstrate making various shaped cones by changing the size of the overlap. Use tape to hold the shapes. Take one cut circle and show where to apply paste. The side that will be underneath will have the paste on the bottom. After the paste has been applied, the cone shape is made and held in place with some pressure until the paste is dry and its shape is held.

7. Challenge the class to make some constructions using cones. Suggest making six or eight same-size cones and clustering them together to create a sphere-like shape. Ask the students to take various-sized square pieces of paper and make a number of different sized and colored cones.

8. Another suggestion is to make a floral form using cones. Take a square piece of paper that will be divided into eight sections. Take a ruler and pencil, and draw lines from opposite corners as before. Fold the opposite sides of the square. This will divide it with fold-and-pencil lines. Fold lines should bisect at the center point. Place the compass point at the center point, and make a circle. Using the circle outline as the outer edge guide, draw scallop shapes that fit in each section. Cut out and finish the cone shapes as before.

9. Now is the time to review the previous lessons. Challenge the students to use cylinders, pyramids and cones to create an interesting construction. It can be an abstract assemblage of geometric forms or one built on a theme, such as rockets, castles, North American Indian tepee villages, airplanes, etc. Students can work alone or in groups. Stress the importance of understanding the concept of volume and the need for good craftsmanship.

The Box or Parallelepiped (grades 4-6)

Let's continue further into more complex volumes and volume constructions. This lesson explores box shapes and the ways to construct them.

1. Review as indicated in other volume sections.
2. Hand out the materials and ask students to cover their desks.
3. Take a piece of 12″ × 18″ construction paper and quickly review how a flat shape can become a three-dimensional form such as a cylinder. Ask the students how it might be made into a box. Discuss parallel lines, and see if they can make the connection between parallel lines and the development of a box. Hold the paper vertically, and then place it on the desk and measure and rule a 1″ line from one of the long-sided edges. Make a fold along this line. Take the other long side and bring it up to the fold. Align carefully and make a fold along the bottom, creating a center fold.

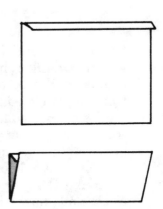

Open the paper. Take the bottom edge to the center fold and make a fold. Turn the paper around and, with the tab folded down, bring the folded edge up to the center fold. You now have a 1″ tab fold at the top and three other folds that create four equal sections.

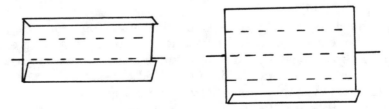

4. Once again, ask the students to determine what these parallel folds on the paper can become. Ask what three-dimensional form could be created. Eventually, one students will come up with the suggestion of an open-ended box.
5. Show students how to carefully apply a thin coat of paste to the tab fold. Apply paste to the top surface. Now bring the bottom edge up and place it over the tab fold. Apply pressure until there is a secure adhesion.

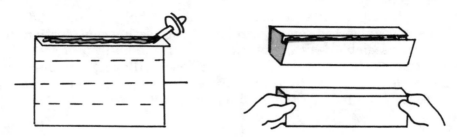

6. Ask the students how they might close the ends. Have them review the closing of the ends of cylinders. Demonstrate how to cut equal scissor lengths at each corner fold. Explain that these cuts will make tab sections to be folded inward to close off the ends.

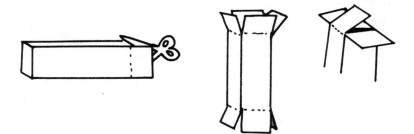

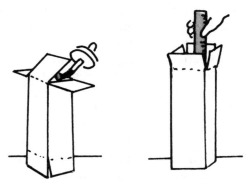

Add white paste to one tab side and bring it over the opposite side. Invert the box on a desktop and put a ruler or hand inside and apply pressure.

The first two sections are now in place. Apply paste to the other two tab sections, fold in place, and apply pressure as before. One end is now closed.

Use the same procedure for the other end, except the final fold over must be done with hand pressure from the top. Do this very carefully with only minimum pressure so that the box will not be crushed. Now everyone has an enclosed box or a parallelepiped.

7. Challenge the students to find box shapes in the classroom. An example would be the room itself, any box or carton, cabinet, milk carton, etc.
8. Now is the time to review all of the previous lessons. Challenge the students

to employ their skills in making cylinders, cones, pyramids, and boxes into exciting creations. Again, a theme such as transportation, outer space, or robots can be used. They may want to make a purely abstract assemblage of the various volumes. Work can be done in groups or individually. After mastering the construction of four-volume forms, the students will be able to suggest many ideas.

The Cube (grades 5-6)

Making a cube requires very careful measuring and assembling. The aim is to produce an object with all sides equal in looks and balance. This nicely enclosed volume has many applications.

1. Continue the same review as suggested in the previous lessons.
2. Review the making of a box, and ask the students what they would do to create a cube. Show a completed cube. They will see that all sides are equal. Introduce the equation formula for determining the volume of a box-like form. For advanced or accelerated students, introduce the volume formulas for cylinders, pyramids, and cones.
3. Hand out the materials and have the students cover their desks.
4. Select a 12″ × 17″ piece of construction paper. Once again, ask students to measure and rule a 1″ line along the top 12″ side. *Measure exactly parallel to the top edge.* Mark off 4″ increments along this line. Do the same along the bottom edge. Connect the points to create two equal-distanced lines, 4″ apart and parallel to the 17″ side. Next, ask students to fold along these lines, one from the left side and one from the right side.

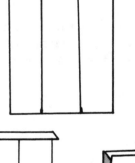

5. The next folds are like those for making the box. Fold the top 1″ line over. Take the bottom edge to the tab fold, align carefully, and fold along the bottom.

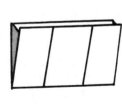

This fold will become the center fold. Next, open the paper and bring the bottom edge up to the center fold.

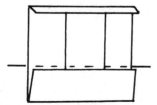

Fold along the bottom. Turn the paper around and with the 1″ tab folded in, bring the fold up to the center fold, and make a fold at the bottom.

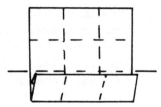

Now the paper should be divided into twelve 4″ squares and three 1″ × 4″ rectangles.

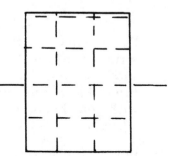

6. Take scissors and cut off the outer two 1″ × 4″ rectangles.

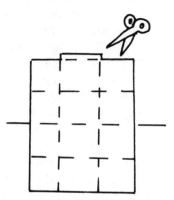

Now there is one section left. Take scissors again and cut each section fold to the pencil lines—*but not beyond.*

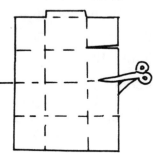

Apply paste on the top of the folded tab and bring up the bottom to it. Apply pressure for adhesion.

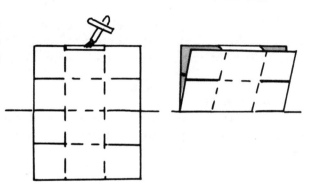

49

7. Now fold in the sides. Fold over one side tab and apply paste. Then overlap with the opposite side. Repeat for the next overlap for the box. Place the hand inside and apply pressure for adhesion.

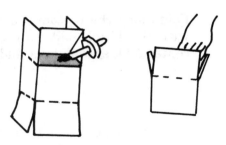

8. Repeat step 7 for the other open end, only this time insert a ruler beneath the first two pasted tabs and apply pressure with your hand. Turn in the third tab and insert the ruler. Paste the fourth flap and gently apply pressure with your hand, as there is no opening. Now the cube is enclosed.

9. Review the success of the project with the class. Again, ask if any cube forms are in the room—ones not noticed before. Challenge the students to plot measurements for making a smaller version of the cube (for example, 9″ × 13″ or 6″ × 9″ paper size).

10. At this time, make a major challenge to the class. Using the volume constructions of cylinders, pyramids, cones, boxes, and cubes, along with supportive decorative accessories, ask students to undertake a full-scale project. With their skills and understanding of volume construction, they can now make impressive-looking projects. Transportation was suggested earlier as a good theme. The age of steam trains could provide a wonderful opportunity to explore the construction of complete trains, which would employ all the volumes learned. Whatever theme is chosen, volume constructions provide an unparalleled opportunity to explore the three-dimensional world and to learn mathematical principles as they relate to flat and three-dimensional shapes.

FOLLOW-UP

Architecture

Devise a major lesson on architecture for the upper grades. Show illustrations of styles and their relationship to the volumes learned. Plan a cityscape, referring to the styles seen today or ones that might be used in the future.

Mathematics

Each step of volume study can be enriched by further math presentations that would coincide with the class level, grouping, or tracking. Volume concepts can be taught with metrics and inches—any method that enhances basic understanding.

Language Arts

Ask students to write stories about the constructions they have made. If it happens to be the Funny Cylinder Person, a history and personality description can be created.

Activity 13 ======================= VOLUMES, PART II—
RECYCLABLE
MATERIALS (K-6)

Recycling is everyone's need for the 1990's and beyond. Reinforce every consumer's need to think about recycling through the use of used objects for the creation of new objects. The projects are also meant to stress the use of creativity and problem solving, while transforming basic volume shapes into new and imaginative-looking objects. This lesson follows Activity 12, "Volumes—Three-Dimensional Art."

OBJECTIVES

Art
- Develop assembling and joining skills.
- Select commonly used materials and assemble them creatively while dealing with problem solving.

Math
- Reinforce math concepts of volume, three dimensions, occupation of space, and measuring skills.
- Identify man-made commercial volumes as to type (cylinder, parallelepiped, cube, etc.).

Science
- Learn about the need to recycle and the methods used to create new products from old ones.
- Learn about energy saved through the use of recyclable materials instead of new raw materials.
- Learn about the environmental impact of garbage and refuse and the need for biodegradable packaging.

History
- Research the use of found objects' collage in the 20th-century schools of art of Dada, Surrealism and Pop.

MATERIALS NEEDED

- Covering for desks
- Scissors
- White glue
- Brushes and sponges
- Tempera paint mixed with liquid dishwashing detergent
- Containers for water

- Paper towels
- Mixed materials for decoration (cotton roving, sequins, buttons, ribbon, wool scraps, fabric scraps, plastic straws, pipe cleaners, colored gum tape, discarded costume jewelry, etc.)

- Scrap colored construction paper
- Pencils and erasers
- Recyclable materials (toilet tissue rolls, paper towel rolls, rinsed plastic bottles, coffee can lids, cereal boxes, aluminum pie pans and cans, plastic packing material, shoeboxes, pill containers, small cardboard jewelry boxes, etc.)
- Brass fasteners, staples, string, etc.
- Spray paint or acrylic paint

PREPARATION

Make several demonstration models in advance. These models will require additional materials before becoming recognizable objects. Let the students provide creative additions to the general forms. You might use the two following basic forms: a plastic gallon milk jug or a shoebox. An endless number of creations can be made from these shapes. Also, in advance, ask the class to collect the items listed under "Materials Needed." Collect visuals that show fine art with various materials as part of the design.

DIRECTIONS

1. Introduce the lesson by raising the issue of the country's over-extended refuse and garbage disposal facilities. Discuss the ways in which many states and communities are handling this problem by developing recycling programs. Introduce discussions about how the children's families can help solve this problem. Ask the students to bring in any local ordinances regarding the disposal of waste. Show examples of fine art that includes various pieces of materials in the design.
2. Ask the students what kinds of materials in the home are recyclable. Make a list on the chalkboard. As the list grows, search in the gathered materials for an example. Talk about the origins of the materials (paper products from trees, aluminum from buxite mines, metal from iron mines, plastics from the petro-chemical industry, etc.).
3. Hold up a variety of forms. Ask the students to identify the volume represented.
4. *For the milk bottle form:* Hold up an empty plastic gallon milk jug. Ask the students to think of what forms in life the jug suggests. List the responses on the chalkboard. Then proceed as follows, challenging the students to guess the identity of the animal to be made.
5. Hold the jug with sides parallel to the table, with the handle pointing upward. Show to the students. Turn the jug upside-down and parallel to the tabletop. Mark off four spots on the cylindrical form at the base equidistant apart. With the scissor point, puncture the plastic carefully at the spots. Insert the cutting edge of the scissors and cut out a circular shape slightly less in diameter than that of the tubes from paper towels or toilet paper. Insert the tubes to desired length—short for a pig, longer for an elephant, etc. As you work, ask the students to guess what animal is being formed.
6. Invert the form and set it on the table. Make all of the legs even. Take the scissors, insert, and make two slits on either side of the handle. Take paper or

cardboard and cut out ear shapes—long and floppy for an elephant or short and pointy for a pig. Insert the ears and ask the students if they recognize the animal form. At this point, they probably will. If so, ask what embellishments can be added to complete the form. The jug opening can become the pig's snout. Eyes, either the store-bought rolling kind or cut out from paper, can now be put in place. Take a pipe cleaner, twist around a pencil to make the pig's curly tail, puncture a hole in the back of the jug and insert the tail. Use a paper tube for an elephant's trunk, and paper for its tail.

7. These forms can be painted with tempera paint mixed with liquid dishwashing detergent. This mix will ensure that the paint will adhere to the various materials used. Experiment with the ratios; although, four parts paint to one part soap is suggested. This should stick to most surfaces. Spray paint or acrylic paint may be used, but its use *must* be monitored. All embellishments should be added *after* the painting has been completed, and they should be attached with white glue.

8. Further embellishments can provide the pig with a humanlike male or female personality. Wrap a female pig with some fabric with lace edging. Shoes can be made from scrap paper or small boxes. Attach cotton roving for the hair. Apply tempera paint for makeup. (See step 7.) Costume jewelry can complete the female pig. For either a female or male pig, wrap colored construction paper around the form to suggest a police officer's or firefighter's uniform. An underwater diver can be made with a swimming suit or trunks, paper flippers on the back feet, gloves on the front feet, and a pair of goggles.

FOLLOW-UP

Art

Note Alexander Calder's use of throwaways. If possible, visit The Mattatuck Museum in Waterbury, Connecticut, and see his tin can toys.

Language Arts

Ask students to prepare written essays and stories about the figures they have created. Have them invent a life for the object, including a name, personality, and lifestyle. Does this figure have a family? Perhaps they can make the family members.

Science

• Have students prepare a research project that illustrates recycling, following the story of the raw product, to the manufactured product, to the used product and its recycled possibilities and saved energy. Explain *biodegradable*.

• Suggest group involvement in a theme project, such as transportation. Using basic forms, construct vehicles such as buses, trucks, campers, and ships. Ask for group reports on engine types, fuel used, and distances covered in a given time.

• Introduce and explain robotics. The students can assemble a series of robot-like figures. They can be humanized like the star of the *Short Circuit* movies, or left looking more like machinery.

• Research how park benches are made from hamburger boxes and plastic foam cups. Find out how soda bottle chips of polyethelene terephthalate can be used to make bathtubs, shower stalls, boat hulls, plastic panels for cars, etc. For more information, write to Rutgers, State University of New Jersey, Center for Plastics Recycling Research, Piscataway, New Jersey 08854.

• Conduct a schoolwide contest for innovative uses for recyclable items—from toys to room heaters (a 12-year-old boy once invented a heater). In 1989 the first contest for recycling aluminum cans was held between the people of New York State and the people of Jiangsu Province, China.

Activity 14 ══════════════════ VOLUMES, PART III— BIG TRUCKS (2-6)

Pay homage to the great trucking industry by building large sized trucks. Do this without any hardship—just collect recyclable materials and start building! Here's a chance to reinforce the concepts of volumes previously explored.

OBJECTIVES

Art
- Learn how to construct large scale, multiple-volume truck forms.
- Make volume size choices.
- Improve and enhance the cutting, pasting, and joining skills.
- Introduce advertising materials as an art form.
- Decorate constructions with advertising materials.

Math
- Reinforce concept of volume and three dimensions through readily available commercial forms.

Geography
- Locate major truck routes on a map.

Language Arts
- Build skills by researching and writing about an important American industry.

MATERIALS NEEDED

The following materials will be needed for each student or group. As these constructions can be rather large, you might want to consider giving this as a group activity.

- Covering for desks or tables
- Pencils and rulers
- White glue, white paste, applicators and rubbing paper
- Scissors, dull kitchen knives, and mat knife (for use by teacher only)
- Poster paint and liquid dishwashing detergent
- #4, #6 and #10 brushes 2" and 3" wide
- Cans of water
- Palettes (coffee can lids or plastic containers)
- Paper towels
- Newspaper to cover floor
- Boxes and corrugated cardboard in all sizes
- Corrugated cardboard sheets cut from very large boxes
- Corrugated cardboard scraps (pieces from boxes)
- Clothesline, rope lengths
- Large brass fasteners
- Advertising materials from magazines and flyers
- ¼" birch dowels in various lengths
- Plastic lids from coffee cans, yogurt, etc.
- Margarine containers in various sizes
- Shoeboxes with lids
- Clear plastic for windshields
- 6" or 8" carpet store tubes
- Paper towel tubes
- Large selection of miscellaneous materials (other plastic lids, square plastic pieces, scraps of tin foil, etc.)
- Small cardboard boxes
- Staplers
- Tape
- Saw
- Plastic pill containers
- Rubber bands

PREPARATION

Partially assemble at least one truck type as a basis to stimulate the children's thinking. Other visual materials would also be useful. (See step 1 under "Directions.") You might try to contact the Teamsters Union, the Interstate Commerce Commission, and/or the American Trucking Association for information regarding their organizations. It would also be useful to obtain several national publications that cater to truckers. In addition, obtain large photos of some of the major rigs encountered on the highway.

DIRECTIONS

1. Hold up an orange, a model of a car, a piece of wood, and initiate a class discussion about these objects' origins. How did they get from where they were made or grown to where they are now? Begin a general talk about transportation and then move on to trucks and the trucking industry. Ask the students what kinds of large trucks they have seen on the roads. Ask on which roads they have seen most of the trucks. Work into a discussion about the country's road system by talking about the Eisenhower Interstate national network of roads, initially built for military purposes but now used by motorists and the trucking industry. Hold up a national road map to see the extent of the system. See who can identify an interstate road. Ask students about their experiences driving on an interstate. Ask about the kinds of trucks they have seen, what they were carrying, their sizes, shapes, etc. Ask someone to come to the chalkboard and draw a common truck shape. The standard form is an 18-wheeler, but some run larger than 24 wheels while others get along with only four. Some newer trucks are tandems.
2. Talk about the two parts of a trailer rig—the cab and the trailer (the payload). Using picture references, discuss the differences in the various types of trucks. Ask students to decide which kind of rig to make. Instead of an enclosed trailer, some may want to make a tank, log, or pipe carrier.

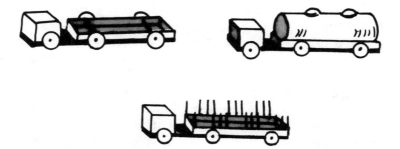

3. To make a large swivel tractor-trailer, select a large corrugated box for the payload. Students who are making an open trailer will cut down the box for a base. The enclosed trailer will have the top open for easy access. This will be sealed before painting. NOTE: Rather than provide all solutions, challenge the students to come up with their own. The lesson is valid as a review and reinforcement for lessons based mostly on mathematics, particularly those stressing volumes and volume construction.

4. For axle holder and reinforcement, measure the box length and width on a sheet of corrugated cardboard. Add flaps that are wide enough to hold a dowel axle and that are about one-third the length of the base. For the reinforcement, just measure the box length and width. Cut out the pieces. Measure, mark, and cut holes for the axles. Make sure they line up correctly.

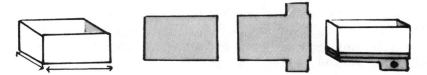

5. Glue the reinforcement to the box bottom. Glue the axle holder to the reinforcement and fold down.
6. Before starting on the cab, refer to cab styles. Use a box that corresponds to the width of the trailer, or cut one to size. If the engine extends in front, use two boxes.

7. Decide now whether to cut out windshields and insert clear plastic, to include seating, dashboard, steering wheel, etc. It's easier to do this before gluing everything closed. If painting on a windshield, complete the cab and trailer first; then paint. If making a see-into cab, complete interior details, including painting, before gluing shut.
8. Now it's time to measure the bed that will hold the cab and axles and slip under the trailer. The measurement will include the cab, the space between the cab and the trailer, plus one-third the length of the trailer. Include flaps for axle holders. Mark for the axle. On another sheet of cardboard, draw the same measurements (without flaps) for the reinforcement. Cut out.

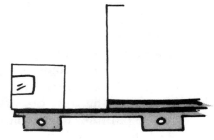

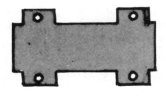

9. Glue the reinforcement to the cab. Glue the axle bed to the reinforcement and fold down the flaps.
10. Measure the axel dowels to size and cut. Supervise this closely.
11. Align all axles and insert into the holes.

12. Plan for wheels. Use plastic coffee can lids, or draw and cut out cardboard wheels. For a heavy load, students may have to use two lids or double cardboard for each wheel. Make center holes. Make them small and adjust to the dowel size. They must fit snugly. Use rubber bands to keep in place.

13. Now you have constructed the two parts of the swivel truck. Take the cab bed and fit it under the trailer. Try out the swivel action and try to approximate where the brass fastener swivel will be placed inside the trailer connecting with the cab bed. Make a mark at that point and punch a hole. Place a pencil point into the hole and work the swivel action with the cab base. Mark the best place for the swivel fastener and punch a hole in the cab bed. Fit the cab base under the trailer and insert the brass fastener.

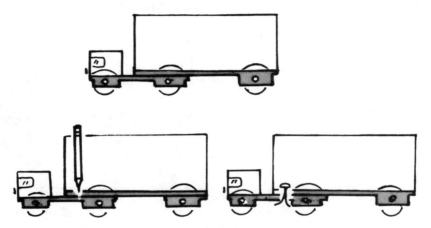

14. Before painting begins, those who chose to make loads of logs, pipes, or tanks will construct these to size. Carpet rolls, paper towel rolls, etc., can be used.

15. Follow the same procedures listed before and monitor these as work progresses. Tell the students to begin with the back and work towards the cab. At each initial phase, stop work and highlight the activity of some group or individual. Emphasize good working habits, good technical skills, good use of scissors, and, of course, using inventive and original ideas. When both cab and trailer are completed, have groups or individuals put these aside until the glue dries overnight.

16. The following day, discuss with the students the way in which their trucks can be painted. Poster paint is best, but this may have to be mixed with dishwashing liquid detergent so that the paint will cover coated stock boxes. Experiment with the amount, although it is usually four parts paint to one part detergent. Review all painting procedures; for example, how to mix the colors, how to apply in neat well-brushed strokes, letting a base coat dry before adding other colors on top for details, etc. The painting should be carefully done, and then allowed to dry overnight.

17. The following day, the students may turn to the various advertising logos or pictures that they have gathered from magazines or received from the organizations listed at the beginning of this activity. These can be cut out and pasted onto the trucks wherever appropriate. Again, review careful cutting and pasting techniques. Rubbing paper here is essential to insure neatness. Gas tanks, exhaust pipes, lights, flaps, horns, power lines, etc., will have to

be attached and painted. Students can select equipment from the supply of foil pieces, fish tank tubing, wire, cans, and other items.

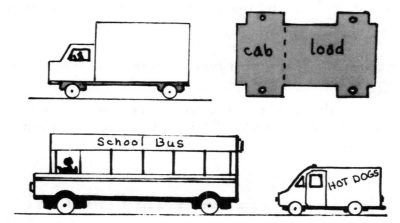

18. To make a large non-swivel base vehicle, choose your payload and cab boxes. Cut to size if needed.
19. Measure the axle base on a sheet of corrugated cardboard. It will include the length and width of the cab and payload. Include flaps and mark the axle holes. Cut a second piece without flaps for reinforcement if needed.
20. Glue the reinforcement to the cab and payload. Glue the axle holder and fold down the flaps. Cut the dowels to size. Measure the axle holes. Be sure they line up, and cut out.
21. Use plastic coffee can lid wheels or corrugated cardboard. Cut to size. Cut the center holes. Make them small and adjust to dowel size. They must fit snugly. Follow steps 15 through 17 to completion.

FOLLOW-UP

Math

As the project progresses, ask students to identify the forms used in the construction of the trucks. Review such terms as cylinder, parallelepiped, cube, etc. Use one model of the truck, display on a board, and pick out the volumes used. See if the load size can be figured mathematically. Construct a payload of small boxes to fit.

Science & Social Studies
• Review the ongoing work on recycling materials. Make a similar display and pinpoint the objects in the construction and define what they are and where they come from; for example, shoebox, plastic juice container, cardboard ice cream container, etc.
• Describe satellite communication between trucker and dispatcher.
• Read about truck stops. A good source is the November 1989 issue of *Smithsonian* Magazine.

Language Arts
• Write to a local trucking company and explain your project. Make a large display in the school lobby. Write reports about each particular truck, the cargo it

carries, and a biography about the driver and his or her family. Invite the trucking company to attend a reception; perhaps the company could supply a speaker to tell the students about the industry. Consider inviting a parent who is a trucker. Photograph the exhibit and send the information to a national trucking publication.

History

Show the transportation in other times with train engines.

Extra Fun Projects

After mastering the basis of construction, the students could make racing cars, solar cars, recreational vehicles (RV's), circus wagons, cement mixers, tractors, sanitation-recycling haulers, etc.

Activity 15 ══════════════════════ PRINT WITH REAL LEAVES (2-6)

This activity has the fun of using a natural object instead of a pencil, brush, or crayon. The students will be very involved with the activity, as it presents many surprising results. It is an exciting introduction to design and printmaking.

OBJECTIVES

Art
- Learn design principles.
- Develop new paint-application skills.
- Use cutting and pasting skills (grades 2-4).

Science
- Learn the importance of leaves in the environment.

MATERIALS NEEDED

- Natural fresh leaves
- Heavy paper for leaf shapes or plastic leaves, when real leaves are not available
- 11″ × 18″ manila or other background paper
- 12″ × 18″ newsprint or other expendable clean paper

60

- Rubbing paper
- Paper towels
- 12″ × 18″ colored backing paper
- Tempera paints
- Coffee can plastic lids for palettes
- Containers of water
- Pencils and erasers
- Scissors
- Paste and applicators
- Brushes or sponges for applying paint on leaves
- Cut-down milk cartons for mixed colors

PREPARATION

Collect fresh leaves. Also have books on hand, such as *Trees* (a Golden Nature Book published by Simon & Schuster) to show leaf shapes and provide information. Be prepared to demonstrate how the leaves are used with the paint. Clean and cutdown milk cartons for mixing colors.

DIRECTIONS

1. Introduce the activity by holding up a leaf and telling the students that this object of nature will enable them to create a colorful design. Point out that the leaf was part of a system that replenishes oxygen, so vital in keeping us alive. Discuss different leaf types, sizes, and shapes. Discuss how a leaf works.
2. Direct the students to get the pressed leaves and lay them on a piece of white paper that will show up their shapes. If real leaves are unavailable, hand out desk covering, pencils, scissors, and paper for the children to make their own leaves, referring to pictures in books. (Or use plastic leaves.)
3. Now the students will be challenged with learning design concepts. Copy these elements of design on the chalkboard:

   a. *Symmetry*—Elements placed in equal proportions, size, color, or weight providing the look of balance.

   b. *Repetition*—The use of the same element again and again.

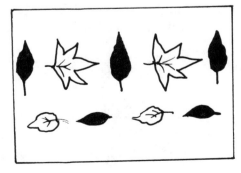

61

c. *Variety*—The use of different elements in a composition. The use of the same element, in which size and placement change.

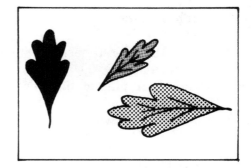

d. *Overlap*—The partial covering of one element over another.

e. *Random design*—The placement of elements in a composition without a formal plan.

f. *Direction*—Movement of design elements.

4. Demonstrate these design possibilities with wet leaves on the chalkboard. Take a leaf, dip it in water, remove excess water, and gently stamp a design on the board. Invite several students to do the same.
5. Hand out the materials, and ask the children to cover their desks.
6. Prepare to demonstrate making a leaf print. Open the tempera jars and stir. The paint should be relatively thick.
7. Mix colors in the milk cartons. They need not be "leaf colors."
8. Demonstrate application of paint on a leaf. Place the leaf, bottom up, on expendable paper. Take a brush or sponge and apply a full yet thin coat of paint. (Do not lose the image of the leaf with excessive paint.)

9. Place the paint-side of the leaf on the background paper.
10. Place the rubbing paper on top and apply hand pressure to insure a good print.

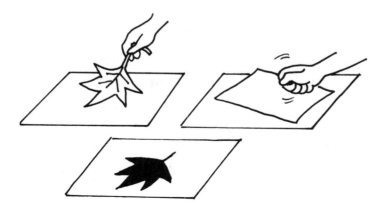

11. Lift the leaf carefully from the background paper surface.
12. Continue the demonstration, using different colors and leaf sizes. For lighter effects, repeat the operation without reapplying paint.
13. Now stop. Ask the students to think about design principles, and begin work in like manner.
14. *For grades 2-4:* Print the leaves, let them dry, and then cut them out. Arrange them in a random or symmetrical design on the background paper. Paste in place, using rubbing paper and hand for good adhesion.
15. After all projects are dry, paste them on the colored backing paper for display.
16. After all work is up for display, invite the students to discuss the results.

FOLLOW-UP

Language Arts

Grades 5 and 6 might use the leaf-print project as a cover for their reports in Activity 20, "Painting Trees in a Seasonal Landscape."

Activity 16 ═══════════════ BARK RUBBING
DESIGNS (4-6)

This is an activity in which everyone will be "barking up the right tree"! On a tree-finding field trip, the children will be surprised by the crayoning results of bark rubbing. Back in the classroom, they will be challenged with creating a nonobjective design with these renderings.

OBJECTIVES

Art
- Introduce texture into design.
- Experience the look and feel of texture.
- Use new and different crayoning skills.
- Learn to make a nonobjective design.
- Use cutting and pasting skills.
- Learn about positive and negative space and shapes.

Science
- Learn that bark is used in medicine, chemicals, and plastics.
- Study the bark and the interior construction of a tree.

MATERIALS NEEDED

- Covering for desks
- Middleweight manila paper in 6″ squares
- Dark brown and black crayons
- Manila or other suitable paper (textured or smooth) for background paper
- 12″ × 18″ colored backing paper
- Black and brown construction paper in 6″ squares

- Pencils
- Scissors
- White paste and applicators
- Rubbing paper for gluing
- NOTE: For teacher demonstration, have a selection of 6″ rubbing squares and 6″ colored squares

PREPARATION

Plan a field trip to a place having a variety of trees. Provide the children with pieces of crayon and plenty of 6″-square manila paper pieces. (Grades 2-6 will need extra paper for use in making "Bark Rubbing Critters" in Activity 17.) Have a whole series of 6″ colored construction squares that can be used for a demonstration prior to the arrangement part of the lesson. Review design principles in Activity 15, step 3.

DIRECTIONS

1. Tell the students that bark is used in the manufacture of medicines, chemicals, and plastics, and give examples. Tell how Native Americans made birch bark canoes.
2. While on the field trip, direct the students to feel the texture of grass, sidewalk, soil, and then the bark of trees. Ask for reactions to the activity. Work towards defining *the art element—texture (how a surface feels)*.

3. After coming to a group of trees, tell the students to watch as you demonstrate how to make a bark rubbing. Place a manila square over the bark surface, hold it firmly in place, and run a crayon over the paper in a vertical manner. This will pick up an impression of the bark's texture. Challenge the students to make a series of at least eight rubbings from different trees. Use different edges of 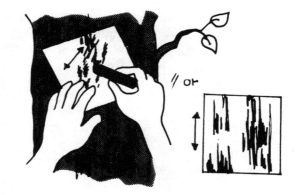 the crayons—flat or point side—and use different pressures for a variety of results. (Grades 2-6 will be making rubbings for their "Bark Rubbing Critters" in Activity 17.)

4. Upon returning to the classroom, select a number of different rubbings and tape them to the chalkboard. Ask the class to discuss the results. Are there any apparent differences in the rubbings? Can we identify individual tree types from these? How does the texture change with each tree type?

5. *Arrangement 1:* Challenge the students to make an arrangement using only their eight 6″ squares. Discuss limitations. Using demonstration pieces already prepared, ask students how they can increase possibilities yet still maintain the shape of the square. As you add more demonstration squares to the board arrangement, ask students how they can increase their numbers without resorting to making additional rubbings. Look for the answer—cutting. Challenge students to cut either nine 2″ squares or thirty-six 1″ squares of the bark rubbings *and* the black and brown squares. Leave some 6″ squares whole. (Employ a math lesson using a ruler.) With these  additional examples, return to the demonstration at the board and ask the students how an arrangement can be made. Make the students note the vertical direction on most bark rubbings. Ask how this can be a factor in making an arrangement. Introduce the concept of repetition—*the repeating of an element.*

Introduce the concept of pattern—*repetition in some prescribed system.* (Review the design principles in Activity 15, step 3.) Send a student to the board, and ask him or her to create an arrangement that uses repetition, pattern, and direction of the rubbing marks. Employ two other design concepts—symmetry and asymmetry. Introduce definitions of both as arrangements are made on the board. Ask the same student at the board to create a symmetrical pattern of repeated shapes.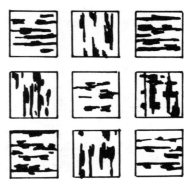

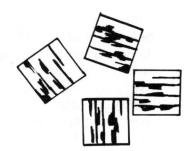

Ask the same student to make an asymmetrical pattern. Add that balance is achieved through use of equal size, shape and position on either side of a dividing line. Asymmetry would show an imbalance.

Introduce the colored construction paper squares. Ask the students how these can be introduced and kept within the framework of the arrangement. Send a student to the board and ask him or her to introduce the colored squares into the arrangement. Again, use the concepts of symmetry and asymmetry.

With the demonstration completed and questions answered, challenge the students to "play" at arranging the group of 1" or 2" squares and adding these to the colored papers. Students should explore a wide range of choices that cover balance, symmetry, use of pattern, etc., as they come to a decision about what will be their final composition. You should circulate about the space calling attention to some products of interest, so that all class members can take advantage of a wealth of possibilities before selecting their final arrangement. When this is done, the students should follow good pasting techniques to affix the squares to the background paper.

6. *Arrangement 2:* While arrangement 1 relies on an orderly arrangement stressing symmetry, challenge the students to make a random arrangement based on asymmetry, incorporating the colored squares or using colored paper as a background for the bark rubbing shapes.

7. *Arrangement 3:* Return to the original eight 6" squares. Ask students to select a colored 6" square and match it up with a rubbing. Now ask for other ways in which to cut the original pieces. Demonstrate that by holding the same-size pieces together and cutting them out, they will obtain shapes of the same size.

Tape a piece of large manila paper to the board. Ask a student to take the two shapes and place them on the manila paper. By placing them opposite each other, you can create a shadow image of the other.

Repeat this several times and continue to ask students to place them on the manila paper. Depending on where the first two were placed, the resulting arrangement can work towards a symmetrical design or one that is asymmetrical. Show another concept—that of positive and negative shapes. The rubbing shape could be the positive shape, while the colored shape could act as a negative shape; or the negative shapes could be those spaces created on the manila background by the cutout shapes. In this instance, it is better not to overlap the shapes but to let the composition develop by having the shapes touch each other.

Design
Negative Space

Arrangement 4 would follow the same basic directions except that this time a random pattern can guide the composition and the student would be free to overlap shapes if he or she chooses to do so.

8. After cutting out the shapes, ask the students to arrange their compositions. Check each one's design progress. When they are satisfied with their bark-rubbing placements, tell them to mark them with their pencils so they can paste them in place. Before pasting occurs, have the students tour the room and view other students' work and generate questions.

9. Instruct the class to apply a small amount of paste to the back of each cut piece and place it where planned on the background paper. Place a piece of rubbing paper on top and rub with the hand to create a smooth neat adhesion.

10. Paste the design on the colored backing paper, and arrange a display. Invite class discussion on the results. Review the concepts. Incorporate the concepts and terms with definitions in the display. Use these in spelling and vocabulary work.

FOLLOW-UP

History

Collect visuals and information on Native American use of birch bark canoes.

Science
- Collect samples of bark and mount a display.
- Study the cross section of a tree.

Activity **17** ══════════════════════ **BARK RUBBING
CRITTERS (2-6)**

This activity lets imagination become the main source of a successful project. The children will be drawing real or imaginary animals living in a tree. Using cutouts from bark rubbings (see Activity 16, step 3), they will then decorate these creatures.

OBJECTIVES

Art

- ◆ Use a lot of imagination.
- ◆ Develop new crayoning skills.
- ◆ Use texture in a design.
- ◆ Improve and strengthen cutting and pasting skills.

MATERIALS NEEDED

- Covering for desks
- Bark rubbings
- Crayons of all colors
- Pencils
- 11″ × 17″ light-colored background paper

- Scissors
- Paste and applicators
- Rubbing paper
- 12″ × 18″ colored backing paper
- Colored paper scraps

PREPARATION

Have the bark rubbings made in Activity 16 on hand. Locate books and magazines with stories and information on animal life in trees. Two such resources are *The World in a Tree* by Stanley Klein (New York: Doubleday, 1974) and "When Disaster Struck a Woodpecker's Home" in the December 1966 issue of *National Geographic* to be read to the students.

DIRECTIONS

1. Introduce the lesson by asking the students what animals live in trees, what animals have they seen living in trees, and what animals couldn't possibly live in a tree. Follow this introduction by reading a story about animals living in a tree.

2. Tell the students that they will create, in crayon, a real or imaginary "critter" that might live in a tree. They will take the bark rubbings made on a field trip, cut them into various shapes, and clothe or decorate the critter. It can be funny, scary, or just a cute critter. It could be a squirrel or a visitor from another planet. It could be part spider and part bird. Tell the students to use a lot of imagination.

3. Ask the students to cover their desks. Hand out 11″ × 17″ background paper and colored scraps.
4. Instruct the children to choose their crayon colors and start to design the critters to fit well into the background space. Stress body parts—head, stomach, legs, etc. It is easier to construct the whole figure first and then glue it to the background. Start with drawing a basic body shape.
5. Tell them to be thinking where they want to put the bark rubbing cutouts. They can be wings, tails, hats, antennae, etc.
6. The body shape will then be cut out and the paper shapes cut to size and shape. Paste these on the body, using rubbing paper on the shapes and rubbing with the hand to insure a good adhesion.
7. Add details—eyes, nose, mouth, etc., using all scrap parts and crayons.
8. When the creature is completed, paste it on the colored background paper and then onto backing paper. Ask the students to name their critter and write its name on the drawing. Display the project around the room for everyone's enjoyment.

FOLLOW-UP

Art

Ask if anyone in the class has a tree house. Discuss how it would feel to live in a tree. Ask if anyone would like to design a tree house on the chalkboard or with paper and crayons or markers.

Activity 18 ══════════════════ MY SPECIAL TREE (K-6)

This stimulating project challenges the children to use their observational skills. A visit to a tree site enables them to study and sketch tree shapes. (This activity can be combined with Activity 16, "Bark Rubbing Designs.") All activities about trees are especially meaningful when used as a theme in April, when all states except Alaska observe Arbor Day. The use of *Discover Trees* by Douglas Florian (New York:

Charles Scribner's Sons, 1986) and the Audubon Society's books helps introduce the subject.

OBJECTIVES

Art
- Sketch from observation and memory.
- Sketch with pencils, crayons, and charcoal.
- Understand size relationships.
- Sketch line and mass.
- Work with light and shadow.

Science
- Identify tree species by bark, shape, and leaves.
- Identify animals and insects dependent on trees.

MATERIALS NEEDED

- Covering for desks
- 8½″ × 11″ paper for outdoors sketch
- Chipboard 9″ × 12″
- Bags for collecting leaves, seeds, etc.
- #2 pencils, black crayons, or charcoal
- 12″ × 18″, 16″ × 20″ or larger drawing paper
- Newspapers, bogus paper, or pads for sitting
- Paper clips

PREPARATION

Plan a field trip to a park, woods, or a tree-lined street. Tell the students in advance that they will be carefully observing tree shapes and sketching one particular tree in detail. Have bags ready for collecting leaves, seeds, blossoms, bark, etc., for class study. Assemble as many visuals as possible, showing tree shapes and seasonal colors. If this activity is to be combined with Activity 16, "Bark Rubbing Designs" or Activity 17, "Bark Rubbing Critters," take along a quantity of 6″ manila paper squares and black crayon pieces.

DIRECTIONS

1. Using the visuals on hand, introduce the students to observing the differences in tree trunk shapes, limb directions and the overall shapes. Tell them they will be sketching tree shapes and that a sketch is a rough or incomplete drawing that conveys basic shapes or ideas.

2. After the students have observed a variety of tree shapes, ask everyone to choose a single tree and study it carefully. This will be the special tree they will sketch. Ask if anyone can identify the kind of tree it is. Hand out seating and drawing materials. Clip drawing paper to chip board with paper clips. Ask the students to start sketching. Stress placement on paper, tree shape, limb direction, leaf masses, root shape at ground level. Students should rough sketch all these points before le ving.

3. Gather any leaves, seeds, blossoms, and bark found, and place them in the bags. Tell everyone to take a last look at the special tree and check its overall shape.

4. After returning to class, select one or more students to sketch a tree or trees from memory on the chalkboard. Ask them to visualize the tree shapes. Were they tall and slender? Were they round and full of leaves? Were the branches massive and high? Or were the branches slender, and did they move in the breeze?

5. Hand out the large drawing paper and the covering for the desks.

6. Direct the students to again draw their special tree with other trees.

7. Caution them to work lightly as they form the picture, using their outdoor sketch for reference. Tell them to make good use of the space. Place trees of various sizes in clumps, or alone, in the background or foreground. When the students are satisfied with the shapes, tell them to go over the selected lines with a darker line to define them.

8. Now is the time to decide on the direction of the light source. The trees should have a light and a dark side and cast a shadow on the ground.

9. Show the class examples of good technique, interesting forms, good value contrasts, and tree shape accuracy. Review texture achieved on bark rubbings, as described in Activity 16.

10. Ask the students their impressions of the field trip. Ask what animals or insects they might have seen in the trees. Ask if they "see" trees differently since the trip.

Science

Create a display of leaves, seeds and blossoms with identification and information.

Activity 19 ════════════════ PAINTING TREES IN A LANDSCAPE (2-6)

This painting project is the next step for students to take after learning to sketch. It will enable them to learn to mix colors and to apply them in a free manner with brushes and sponges. Studying landscapes painted by the masters can help students understand landscape painting and appreciate fine art.

OBJECTIVES

Art
  * Study the landscape paintings of the masters.
  * Understand the elements of a landscape.
  * Learn to mix tempera colors.
  * Develop the use of brushes and sponges.
  * Paint different tonal qualities.

Language Arts
  * Write an essay.
  * Use descriptive writing or verbal skills.

MATERIALS NEEDED

  * Covering for desks
  * Pencils or chalk
  * Containers of water
  * Plastic dish palettes
  * Paste and applicators
  * Paper towels
  * 17″ × 21″ and 18″ × 24″ colored backing paper
  * Tempera paints
  * Cut-down milk cartons for mixing colors
  * #2, #7, and #10 brushes
  * Sponge pieces
  * 16″ × 20″ and 17″ × 23″ heavy paper
  * Paper scraps for color testing

PREPARATION

Assemble audio-visual materials about landscape painting, as well as prints and magazine pictures. Include such examples as medieval manuscripts, Chinese scroll and screen paintings, as well as landscapes by Corot, Constable, Giorgione,

Turner, Cole, Bierstadt, Church, Kensett, Cézanne, Monet, and Van Gogh. Wash and cut down milk cartons for mixing paints. See lesson on looking at pictures, Activity 9.

DIRECTIONS

1. Introduce the lesson by telling the children that they will be creating a painting in steps that were used by the masters. They will be planning to paint sky, land, and trees. There will be masses of color, lights, and darks, and some details painted with brushes and sponges.

2. Show assembled visuals. Discuss the landscape composition. Point out the use of a center of interest and the breakdown of the foreground, middleground, and background. Stress the individuality of each artist's work.

3. Write this representative landscape color guide on the chalkboard (A Van Gogh scheme will be different):
   a. *Ground area*—tan to dark brown, light to dark greens (mix these colors first)
   b. *Sky*—blue and white
   c. *Tree trunks and limbs*—light tan, browns, and black
   d. *Leaves*—light yellow-green to dark blue-green

4. Review color mixing. (See Activity 4, "Rainbows and Watercolors.") The following are the colors most used in this activity:
   a. Light tan = yellow + some red + little blue
   b. Brown = equal amounts of red and yellow + some blue + black
   c. Yellow-green = yellow + little blue
   d. Blue-green = yellow + blue + touch of black

5. Hand out the materials and ask the students to cover their desks. Instruct the students to sketch in their compositions lightly, using pencil or chalk. Remind them to make good use of the space and draw the shapes of trees they have observed. When the sketching is completed, have the students review the sketches and suggest changes. Ground levels may need to be changed or a center of interest made larger. Encourage students to use their imagination as well as their observational skills. Remind them that the trees in the distance will be smaller and that by varying the types of trees they will create an interesting composition. Also include dead trees and branches for contrast.

6. Hand out the rest of the materials. Ask those who would like to mix the colors to take the milk cartons and paints and begin making batches of the colors suggested on the chalkboard. Mix the sky colors first. Students will take some of the paint and put it on their palettes.

7. Now tell the students to paint in the sky area with big broad strokes.

8. After the sky is blocked in, begin painting the ground. The darker areas will be in the foreground and the lighter ones in the distance. However, when each area is broken up into lighter and darker areas, the painting will have more design interest. Let it dry.

9. Now the painting of the trees can begin. Keep reminding the children to paint in a loose, free manner, especially the leaf masses.

10. Consider the light source, and paint the shadows on the trees accordingly. Hold off on details. Let dry.

11. When dry, tell the students that *now* details are needed. They can take semi-dry sponge pieces or a dry brush to apply paint to the clouds and foliage, giving them texture. Simulate bark and add grasses. Then add animals and birds.

12. After the pictures are dry, assemble the landscapes around the room and ask the students' opinions on the work done. Review the concepts of texture, mass, shadows, etc.

13. Tell the children to continue work and observe the suggestions made by the class.

14. Upon completion, ask the students to choose a piece of colored paper that would best complement the picture. Take the landscape and paste it on the backing paper, ready for display.

FOLLOW-UP

Art

- Repeat the lesson, using Van Gogh's styles and colors

Language Arts

- Write an essay about the impact of trees on our lives.
- Give an oral presentation describing painting trees. Or describe trees in writing.
- Research an artist from the print group, and write a brief biography.

PAINTING TREES IN A SEASONAL LANDSCAPE (2-6)

This activity should follow Activity 19, "Painting Trees in a Landscape." The children will be challenged to paint a new landscape theme with seasonal colors and shapes. Use this activity to motivate the students to read maps, gather research, and write reports and essays.

OBJECTIVES

Art
+ Learn landscape painting.
+ Mix colors.
+ Paint in a loose, free manner.

Science
+ Study the life cycle of trees.
+ Study forests.

Social Studies
+ Study nutrition.
+ Learn about products made from trees.
+ Learn about the endangered forests of the world.
+ Study the people who live in rain forests.

Language Arts
+ Write reports and essays.

MATERIALS NEEDED

- Covering for desks
- 12″ × 18″ or 16″ × 20″ paper
- Pencils or chalk
- Tempera paints
- Crayons and markers
- Cut-down milk cartons
- 13″ × 19″ or 17″ × 21″ colored backing paper
- Maps of the U.S.
- Sponge pieces

- Plastic coffee can lid palettes
- #2, #7, and #10 paintbrushes
- Water jars
- Paste

PREPARATION

Make a copy of the U.S. map (don't forget Hawaii and Alaska) for each student or group.

DIRECTIONS

1. Introduce the lesson by telling the students that they will have a choice of painting a spring, summer, fall, or winter landscape. Inform them that trees in each season have a different silhouette and the leaves have different colors. In winter, the trees are bare of leaves. These changes occur in certain parts of the U.S. Ask the class if anyone can locate these areas on a wall map. If the students are in one of these areas, ask them to choose a tree outside the classroom and record its changes by drawing them throughout the year. Show the students as many visuals as possible of the seasonal changes.
2. Explain to the students that these changes occur as part of the life cycle of trees. On the chalkboard, copy the illustrations of an apple tree's seasonal cycle. As you point out the progress of the bud to blossom to fruit to seed to new tree, ask a student to show an example from collected tree objects or visuals.

3. Hand out the copies of the U.S. map and crayons, asking the children to mark the main fruit- and nut-growing regions as you point them out on a wall map. Also ask students to draw pictures of the crops that are grown for market.
4. Ask the students if anyone can tell about the benefits of eating fruit and drinking the juice.
5. Since fruit trees are just a small part of the number of trees in this country, ask the students what other kinds of trees grow in the U.S. Tell them that many forests and woods are in danger of disappearing through pollution, fire, and other factors. Ask if anyone has been camping or hiking in a forest or wood. Invite them to tell what it looked like and how they felt about it.
6. Now the students can begin their painting activity by choosing the season they wish to paint.

7. Copy this color guide on the chalkboard:
   a. *Spring*— light greens, yellow-greens
         yellows
         pinks
         white
   b. *Summer*—dark greens, middle-value greens
         reddish-greens
         yellows
         yellow-greens
         reds
   c. *Fall*— oranges
         reds
         reddish-browns
         dull greens
         yellows
   d. *Winter*— white
         blues
         violet
         tan
         black

8. Hand out the materials and ask the students to cover their desks.
9. Take the tempera paints and ask the students to mix the paint in seasonal color groups in the milk cartons.

10. Instruct the students to begin their sketching with pencil or chalk, reminding them to make good use of the space and that the tree shapes are the most important elements of the composition.

Yes

No

11. Before painting begins, ask the students' opinions on the sketches. Ask if any changes should be made.
12. Tell the students to begin painting the sky area first in broad free strokes, as they did in the previous activity. Tell them to continue by next painting the ground with a #7 or #10 brush, and then the trees. Refer to the color guide in selecting the seasonal colors.

13. Consider the light source direction and paint shadow areas accordingly. Apply semi-moist sponge pieces for foliage detail and wispy clouds.

14. Tell the students to add such details as blossoms, fruit, grasses, rocks, birds, and other animals. Persuade them to use imaginative and individual touches, using sponge and "dry" brushwork.
15. Let the completed work dry on the desks. Then add extra touches in crayon and markers.
16. Paste the landscapes onto colored backing paper and display.

FOLLOW-UP FOR GRADES 5-6

Language Arts

This is a report or essay project that includes a topic relating to social studies or the arts. These reports can be read to the students. The essays and reports can be kept in a folder made from the leaf print project in Activity 15, "Print with Real Leaves."

Suggested topics are:

- International forest products and their transportation to the U.S.
- Endangered rain forests and how to save them.
- Life of the tribes in the Philippine rain forests.
- New uses for wood in high-tech industry.
- Wood products in the home—from safety matches to cedar closets.
- How to control tree pests.
- U.S. fruit and nut crops.
- How tree rings help scientists date objects as old as the Ice Age.
- The building industry's use of lumber.
- How wood is used in making furniture and musical instruments.
- How wood is used in making sports equipment, such as baseball bats, boats, oars, golf clubs, hiking and hockey sticks, pool cues, croquet sets, and bowling alleys.
- The art of woodcarving from fine art to whirligigs, to whittling and American Indian totem poles, to homemade pegs.
- Trees—homes to insects, birds, and other animals.
- How can we preserve a local historical tree like the Ancient Oak of Charleston, South Carolina or the General Sherman Sequoia of California.
- How I'd design a super tree house.
- Why trees are needed for oxygen, wildlife protection, and soil stability.

Some information sources include the following articles in *National Geographic:*

- "Stone Age Men of the Philippines" (August 1972)
- "Ozark Woodcarvers" (July 1975)
- "Twilight of Hope for Big Cypress" (August 1976)
- "Our National Parks" (July 1966 and July 1979)
- "Rain Forests" (January 1983)
- "Isle Royale—North Woods Park Primeval" (April 1985)

Activity 21 ================ COPYING IN CLAY (K-6)

Creating a recognizable copy of an object while wearing a blindfold can be a challenging learning experience. Students will discover a "new dimension" of volume study.

OBJECTIVES

Art
- Experience the forming of a volume with a solid material.
- Become acquainted with clay modeling.
- Learn to connect touching and mental images.
- Increase coordination skills.

MATERIALS NEEDED

- Covering for tables or desks
- Clay or plasticene
- Water to moisten clay and clean hands
- Paper towels
- Blindfolds
- Simple shaped objects (book, plastic animals such as dog, cat, dinosaur), etc.

PREPARATION

Depending on the time available and size of the class, decide whether every student will have an opportunity to be involved in the modeling or whether students will volunteer. Try to guide those students who would especially benefit from this exercise to be active participants. Keep selected objects to be copied out of sight.

DIRECTIONS

1. Cover one desk or table and ask the students to gather around it.
2. Tell the students that they will be using their sense of touch, imagination,

and their understanding of volume as they feel an object and copy it in clay.

3. Blindfold a student and hand him or her an object, asking him or her to carefully study the shape and overall volume or space it occupies.
4. After the student has studied the object, ask him or her to try to copy it with the clay.
5. After the modeling has been completed, ask the student to look and criticize the results. Ask the student to point out where the work is successful and where there is some need for further work and understanding. Also ask how it felt to work in this manner. Encourage the other students to ask questions about the process.

Activity 22 ============ CLAY HAND PRINTS FOR PARENTS (K-1)

A simple clay project that all parents will cherish is the print of their child's hand cast permanently in a hard ceramic material. These make great Mother's Day, Father's Day, holiday, and birthday presents.

OBJECTIVES

Art
 • Learn about one use of a plastic material.
 • Become acquainted with clay and how it changes shape.
 • Learn manipulative skills to shape clay.

Science
 • Learn about the properties of a major and very old material that has many uses in the world around us.

MATERIALS NEEDED

 • Covering for desks
 • Ceramic clay (Indian red or Jordan) the size of an orange
 • Kiln (to be used only by an adult)
 • Pencils and erasers
 • Old toothbrushes (optional)
 • Water in small dishes
 • Shoe polish and brushes
 • Wood backing, sandpaper
 • White glue

PREPARATION

Prepare clay balls ahead of time. Obtain scrap wood pieces for mounting from a lumberyard or obtain precut pieces from the same source. Have available several clay pieces in different states. Arrange for kiln use.

DIRECTIONS

1. Take a piece of scrap clay and ask the students about its use. Ask them to touch the clay and discuss how it feels and looks. Hold up several common objects such as a flower pot, a tile, a dish, and a brick, and ask the students what material these are made from. Tell about how long mankind has used the material and how useful it is to people in their lives. Take another piece of clay and press it into a shape. Show another piece that has hardened, one that has dried, and still another that has been fired.

2. Ask the students if they've heard their parents or siblings complain about their dirty hands. Through class discussion, bring the conversation around to the washing of hands and what happens if you touch walls with dirty hands. Invite the students to make a memento of their hands so that their parents will never forget them nor their hands!

3. Distribute clay balls to all students. Show them how to pat the ball into an oblong pancake shape. Check the results. Students will be more interested in making other things with the clay. Attempt to create an even, smooth surface the size of which should fit both hands. (If this is not possible, then work for one hand.)

4. When the oval shape has been completed, ask students to place their hand or hands onto the clay. It is important that there be sufficient clay left around each hand. Leaving one hand on the clay, tell each student to take the other hand and press the same into the clay. Walk around the  space and give assistance and pressure wherever needed. Carefully remove the hand. Repeat with the other hand. *It is important to obtain as much detail as possible.* When the image of one or both hands has been completed, wet a finger with some water and smooth out the edge of the oval shape. Along the edge or in spaces not occupied by the hand image, have students print their name with a pencil point. Put the date on the chalkboard, and have them copy it in another space.

5. Allow the oval shape to set before removing to a very dry storage area prior to firing. Prints should dry *at least two weeks or more* until you are assured that no moisture remains. Stack the ovals in a kiln and slowly fire to cone 05 or 06 about 1950 degrees.

6. When the firing has been completed and the shapes are cool, they can be distributed to the students. Liquid or wax shoe polish can be applied, allowed to dry, and the shape then buffed with a brush. You might want to use an old toothbrush to force polish into grooves.

7. Buffing will create a mellow glow and shine to the hand shapes. These can then be glued with white adhesive to wood pieces, which have been sanded.

FOLLOW-UP

Set up a display for Parents' Night and have students place their hand images on their desks to surprise parents who visit.

Activity **23** ══════════ **PLASTICENE PRINTING (1-2)**

Combine the fun of printing with the fun of modeling with plasticene.

OBJECTIVES

Art
- Model free forms.
- Improve manipulative skills.
- Learn basic print techniques.
- Learn design planning.

MATERIALS NEEDED

- Covering for desks
- Plasticene
- Milk cartons for paint
- Thick tempera paints in various colors
- #6 and #7 paintbrushes
- Paste and applicators

- Paper towels
- Coffee can lid palettes
- 20-lb or 16-lb white paper cut to size
- Colored backing paper 1″ larger than white paper
- Rubbing paper

PREPARATION

Cut paper to size, and collect coffee can lids. Collect and wash milk cartons for paint.

DIRECTIONS

1. Distribute materials, and ask students to cover their desks.
2. Pour the paints into the milk cartons and mix the paint to a creamy consistancy.
3. Tell the students to take a piece of plasticene and roll it out into a rope.
4. Continue by modeling a free form shape approximately 2″ wide. Then attach areas and firmly press together. Continue to make other free forms. Smooth out any lines.

5. Take some paint and mix it on the lid palette. Caution the children that when they make the color choice for their print form, the same color paint must be used each time more paint is applied.

6. Check the students' palettes to see that the paint is not runny. Then ask the children to take the form in one hand and apply the paint with a brush. Brush away any drips. Cover the entire bottom surface.

7. Next, tell everyone to wipe their fingers and then press the form onto the paper surface using rubbing paper on top. Lift immediately.

8. Let the students decide where to paint succeeding color forms. Show them that they can overlap the prints. Use activities 15 and 16 for design and arrangement ideas.

9. After the printing is completed, mount it on the colored backing paper and display.

FOLLOW-UP

Art

• For holiday motifs, the plasticene forms can be hearts, shamrocks, Christmas trees, etc. Try printing with vegetables or fruits. Use the same method of printing, only use cut foods such as broccoli, green peppers, onions, oranges, and apples. You can also use such found objects as spools, sponges, erasers, etc.

• Make patterns of simple shapes and cut household sponges to shape. Use with plasticene printing for added interest in texture.

Activity 24 ══════════ LINE DESIGN PRINTING (1-3)

Younger children will enjoy this introduction to printing. It will be fun to arrange yarn or string in various shapes, paste them on cardboard, and print in different colors. Keep this lesson in mind around gift-giving time, when students can make attractive printed wrapping paper.

OBJECTIVES

Art

♦ Use manipulative skills.
♦ Improve pasting skills.
♦ Learn linear arrangement.

- Make and use artwork as a tool.
- Introduce printmaking.
- Learn direction, repetition, etc.

History
- Learn the story of printing.

MATERIALS NEEDED

- Covering for desks
- Chipboard, heavy cardboard, pad back, etc., cut to size
- Absorbent cotton string or wool yarn (no acrylics)
- #4 and #6 paintbrushes
- Colored construction paper for backing
- Paper towels

- White glue
- Scissors
- Thick tempera paint
- Coffee can lids for palettes
- 20-lb or 16-lb white paper or typing paper cut to size
- Bristle brushes for spatter work
- Pencils and erasers

PREPARATION

Cut the cardboard and white paper to size, or obtain typing paper. Plan for two lesson sessions. The first session is for constructing the printing stamp, allowing drying time to secure the string or yarn for printing. For the second session, arrange the students in groups so that they have easy access to various paint colors and can exchange printing stamps. Collect a lot of lids for paint palettes and any information on printing methods and history. Refer to Activity 15, "Print with Real Leaves," for composition tips.

DIRECTIONS

1. Hand out the covering for desks, cardboard, pencils, scissors, yarn, and glue.
2. Take a piece of cardboard and demonstrate that a design can be a simple free form or a geometric shape. Ask the students to draw their ideas on their cardboards. Check the students' work, making sure the string or yarn can follow the line and be glued in place easily.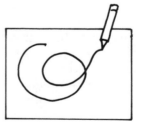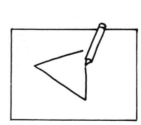
3. Show how to squeeze the white glue and guide the tip along the drawn lines. Tell the students to do the same and carefully lay the string or yarn on the glue, pressing lightly. Cut the yarn to size. Let the print stamps dry thoroughly.
4. Preparation for the printing session includes grouping the desks and handing out the materials (covering, dry printing stamps, paints, brushes, paper, palettes, backing paper and glue).

5. Refer to Activity 15, "Print with Real Leaves," to demonstrate the use of direction, repetition, etc.

6. After the desks are readied, transfer *thick* tempera paint onto the lid palettes. Demonstrate how to put the brushes into the paint (don't overload) and apply them to the string or yarn. Be sure to tell the students to use the same color when reapplying paint. A stamp that starts out yellow must continue being yellow no matter who is using it. Encourage the sharing of stamps for greater design possibilities. After the paint has been applied, turn the stamp over and press firmly on the paper. Remove carefully. Ask the students to do the same.

7. Circulate around the work space and give help where needed. Tell the students to change direction of the stamp on successive printings. Use spatter or stipple (see Activity 4, "Rainbows and Watercolors") to add to the design. Review repetition.

8. After the work is completed and the stamps are dry, glue them onto the colored backing paper and put on display. Encourage a class discussion about how it felt to use this "different" method of applying paint.

FOLLOW-UP

Art

• Make more complicated line designs such as shapes of animals, flowers, letters, or numbers.

• Design wrapping paper prints for gifts at Christmas, Hanukkah, Mother's Day, Father's Day, Valentine's Day, birthdays, etc. Use large sheets of 20-lb or 16-lb white paper.

• Contact a local art association, and ask a printmaker to visit the class and show his or her work and the printing process.

History

Study the highlights of the history of printing—from before the Gutenberg Bible to computer printouts.

Activity 25 ══════════════════ FOUND OBJECT PRINTMAKING—PATTERN AND REPETITION (K-6)

This project is an introduction to printmaking and is made exciting by printing with found objects. It teaches repetition in a set pattern. This concept is used in the world of decorative arts such as textiles, wallpaper, and wrapping paper, where long lengths of the design are needed.

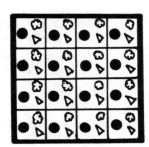

OBJECTIVES

Art
- Learn about the principles of pattern, repetition, balance and sequence.
- Understand the application of studio work to the applied arts.
- Learn how textile designs rely on design principles and elements.
- Learn about multiple images—the first explorations of printmaking.
- Improve manipulative skills.

History
- Gain knowledge about the textile world of today and times past.
- Discover how textiles and wall coverings are designed and made.

Music
- See how some art and musical theory interrelate.

Math
- Improve measuring skills.

MATERIALS NEEDED

- Covering for desks
- Pencils
- Tempera paint
- Brushes in assorted sizes
- Paper towels
- Water containers
- White glue
- Coffee can lid pallettes

- 16″ × 16″ 80-lb white or colored construction paper
- 18″ × 18″ backing paper
- Found wooden objects with one flat side (thread spools, cut wood pieces, knobs, beads, etc.)
- Other small found objects

For Teacher
- music source
- textile/wall covering samples

PREPARATION

Gather together examples of textile and wall coverings. Select those in which the pattern and/or repeat is very obvious. Take one and, using a ruler, separate the repetitions. Review structure and concepts in lesson on geometric designs. Samples can be obtained from wallpaper stores' discontinued designs and ends of rolls. Gift wrapping paper can also be used. Collect found objects.

DIRECTIONS

1. Refer to the first three steps in Activity 8, "Geometric Designs." Repeat or adapt the first three steps listed. Start by rapidly clapping or use foot stomping, singing and repeating a single note. Whatever you select, the emphasis is on the repetition of a sound in a modulated, controlled manner. Compare the random design of Jackson Pollock to the samples of wallpaper or textiles that have controlled sequences.
2. Same as step 2 in Activity 8.
3. Same as step 3 in Activity 8.

4. Draw another square on the chalkboard. Take one of the larger flat found objects and ask a student to do the same operation by wetting the found object and making the impressions on the board. *Reinforce sequence, spacing, and repetition.*

5. Attach a piece of paper to the board. Ready one color of *thick* paint. Ask the students how the same operation could be done with the paint and paper as with the water on the board. Demonstrate the correct procedures for applying the paint to the surface of the found object. Use a brush and charge with a small amount of paint, then press the object onto the paper. Ask a student to try a random pattern. Ask if he or she can create one using the found object and one color of paint.

6. Review other systems, such as the controlled predictable pattern. Ask students how they could better control the placement of color, so that they could obtain the look of the wallcovering or textile; that is, how to repeat the colors and marks in an exact predictable manner. Suggestions will include that one can draw lines like a grid. Counter with suggestions that the paper can be folded. Another suggestion is to select a square piece of paper (although it can be a rectangle) and then fold it into equal-sized squares. A 16″ square will create sixteen 4″ squares. So fold the paper in half, making sure the edges line up. Open the paper. Fold the bottom edge to the center. Fold the other edge to the center. Turn the paper to the side and repeat. This will create sixteen 4″ squares. (Older students can create sixty-four squares.) Fold the bottom up to the center and then fold over again.

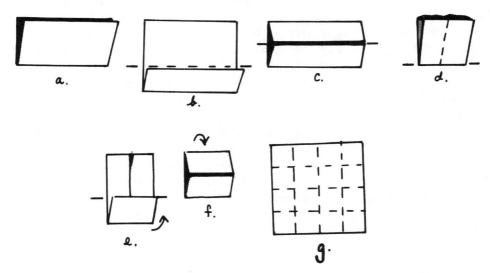

7. Attach two pieces of this folded paper to the board. Use the 4″ squares for demonstration purposes. Select a found object, apply paint by forming a correct sequence (meaning the repeated shape will appear in exactly the same position in each box). Then casually wander from the spot and ignore the sequence. Stop and ask the students what happened. Ask them how to avoid this error. NOTE: It is best if the students choose the spot in each square where that color shape will go. They should follow through with that shape until one appears in each box.

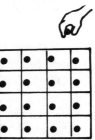

87

Put up another piece of paper. This time, add too much paint. Demonstrate what happens when excessive paint is pushed out by pressure to create an unintended shape of its own.

Use the correct amount of paint to avoid this. Continue the demonstration by showing what happens when the paint is too thin and not enough has been applied. Remember that the intensity of the color is as important as its placement in a controlled pattern.

8. Put up another piece of paper. *For older students,* the problem can be made more complex. Rather than repeat the same shapes and colors in each square, they might want to vary the format and work in a 1-2-1-2-1-2 sequence. This means that every other box will differ. In this case, too, refer to steps 4 and 5 in Activity 8. Teach younger children sequence and space with the simple single square.

9. At this point, let the students select their own background colors and paint colors. Again, refer to the color theory in Activity 4, if you want to stress color, or simply let the students choose their favorite contrasting colors.

10. Distribute supplies and cover tables. Group the tables so that students can share the paint. The first step is to fold the paper as in step 6. Leave the brushes in the paint. Let the students begin to very carefully monitor the first shape and its placement. After a few moments, stop work and review progress. Hold up work that is going well. Give assistance where needed. Then let the work continue. Stop occasionally as work progresses. Review the concept of overlap that can be used in these designs.

11. As work draws to an end, have the students stop work and walk about the area to review the progress of others. Have them then complete their own. Let dry. Have students choose a contrasting color for the backing and display. Students can add glitter, foil pieces, and found objects if desired.
NOTE: Applying paint to an object held in the fingers can be messy for younger students, so monitor this carefully. Have everyone wash up at the end.

FOLLOW-UP

Art

• Extend the lesson so that several designs are made. Introduce the lesson as a project for making wrapping paper that the students can use to wrap presents.

• Create placemats for a parent-school function.

• Use the designs as coverings for books.

• Prepare a display of actual wall coverings and contrast them with the students' work. Demonstrate the useful aspects of this type of artwork and how it is translated to applied fields. Show magazine pictures of interiors with wallpaper, draperies, sheets, etc.

Language Arts

Older students can prepare reports on some aspect of the textile design industry or how wallpapers are made. The reports can also be displayed with the artwork. (See Activity 47, "Fun with Fiber Weaving," for industry sources.)

Activity **26** ══════════════════ HAPPY HALLOWEEN MASKS (K-6)

This project generates enthusiasm long before the actual work begins. The freedom to make monsters, movie stars, or mischievous creatures appear in class on Halloween is very appealing. Grades K-2 can make simple masks from a paper plate base, while the upper grades can make papier-mâché masks. After the Halloween festivities are over, the masks can decorate the classroom or the students' rooms at home. The project is a good beginning exercise for modeling skills. It is also a three-dimensional study that can be applied to almost any theme.

OBJECTIVES

Art
- Learn modeling skills and work in dimension.
- Learn challenging pasting skills making papier-mâché.
- Learn size relationships.
- Use imagination in choice of theme and decoration.

History
- Learn about the thirty thousand-year-old history of mask use in the world.

Social Studies
- Become aware that masks are worn on various occasions today.

Language Arts
- Develop research and descriptive report-writing skills.
- Write a short play.

Geography
- Locate on a world map those places where masks have been popular for many years (Japan, Siberia, Alaska, Puerto Rico, Africa, New Guinea, and South America).

MATERIALS NEEDED:

- Covering for desks
- Paper plates for lower grades
- Plasticene for upper grades
- Newspaper, including color sections; or white and colored paper towels
- Heavy paper
- Large containers for paste mix
- Small containers for paste and water
- Flour and water for papier-mâché paste
- Coffee can lids for palettes
- Staplers

- #2, #3, #10, and #17 brushes
- Tempera paints
- Scissors
- White paste and applicators
- White glue
- Colored construction paper
- Wool, string, beads, dried leaves, husks, feathers, foil, glitter, etc., for accessories
- Rubbing paper
- Elastic or string
- Pencils and erasers
- Markers
- Sandpaper

PREPARATION

Tell the students ahead of time to choose their mask theme and to collect the accessories for their masks. Mix the paste ahead but just before class begins so that it doesn't dry out. Tear newspaper into 1½" strips, or use torn pieces of paper towels, which can work even better. It is easier to keep track of the number of layers when using different colors. Tear enough for six layers per mask. Keep the black-and-white newspaper strips and the color strips separate. Plan time for the papier-mâché to dry thoroughly before painting. If possible, have on hand the following *National Geographic* articles showing masks of various cultures: "Africa Adorned," November 1984; "Living Theater in New Guinea's Highlands," August 1983; "Peoples of the Arctic—Art of the Bering Sea," February 1983. These articles will help inspire design work and increase students' knowledge of the folkways of different cultures.

DIRECTIONS

1. Depending on grade level, introduce the project by telling the students that they will be making masks just as people of all continents have been doing for thirty thousand years. Papier-mâché masks, which they will be making, have been used in the Orient and South America for ages. Some of the oldest existing masks have been found in Japan. Show them any research material and examples of the Greek masks of comedy and tragedy, etc. (theater advertisements usually use them).

2. Hand out the materials and ask the students to cover their desks. Lower grades will be using paper plates, pencils, white glue, scissors, paint or markers, brushes, accessories, and colored paper scraps. Upper grades will be using plain paper, pencils, containers for paste, newspaper or towel strips, and plasticene, paintbrushes, and markers.

3. Lower grades will determine where the eyes, nose and mouth will be placed, marked, and cut out. After that is done, cut paper, straws, buttons, wool, etc., can be glued onto the mask. Attach string to the mask for fastening.

4. Upper grades will need plain paper, pencil, ruler, and plasticene to start their project.

5. Ask students to measure the length of their faces—chin to top of the forehead. Make similar measurement on paper and draw a face oval.

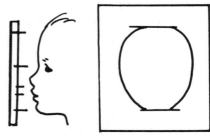

6. Place plasticene on the oval and model into the shape desired. Add features.

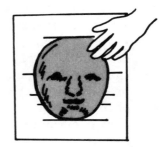

7. Hand out the containers for paste and water, and fill. Hand out torn newspaper or paper towels, keeping black-and-white newspaper strips separate from color newspaper strips, and white paper towel strips separate from colored paper towel strips.

8. The paste should have the consistency of pea soup—thick, and not runny—and be placed in individual containers. Containers of water should be at each desk.

9. Ask the students to follow along as you work. The first layer of paper will be wet strips. *Do not add paste.* Lay black-and-white strips on the plasticene shape, interlocking the strips where possible. Fully cover the plasticene.

10. To keep track of the layers, use black-and-white newspaper strips and then color strips, then black-and-white, then color, etc. (or alternate strips of white paper towel with strips of colored paper towel). Add paste to the color strips and apply over the first layer, fully covering it. Smooth surface with finger and remove excess paste.

11. After the *sixth* layer has been completed, let the mask dry naturally, away from heat.
12. When the mask is dry, carefully remove the molded paper from the plasticene.
13. After the mask is removed, trim ragged edges with scissors. Cut out eyes, nostrils, and mouth. Ask the students to try on their masks and check to see if they can see and breathe without difficulty. If any openings need enlarging, use the scissors to carefully cut away the openings to size. Use sandpaper on rough spots.
14. Distribute paints, brushes, and coffee can lid palettes.
15. Ask the students to begin painting their masks. Tell them to cover the papier-mâché with a base coat color, adding details after the base coat has covered all overlaps of the paper.

16. After the paint has dried, hand out the collected accessories and the white glue. Now the students can put the finishing touches on the masks.
17. There are several choices in making the mask wearable. The first is taking strips of durable paper such as oaktag, and staple the strips to the mask. Another possibility is to make holes in the mask and tie elastic or string to it. If there are any objections to the students wearing the masks, tape tongue depressors or ice cream sticks or dowel sticks to the masks to hold them in front of the face.
18. Now everyone is ready for the class party or school parade. After the festivities are over, the masks can decorate the room or be taken home to decorate the students' rooms.

FOLLOW-UP

Art and Language Arts

• Research the African wooden masks of the Ivory Coast, and write a report. Show visuals that illustrate how these masks influenced 20th-century painters.

• Create a short play that calls for the making of masks. It could be an adaptation of an old fable or an original work. Recall mask wearing in ancient Greek play presentations.

• Write reports on and show examples of Native American masks.
   a. *Northwest Coast*—animal masks with movable jaws worked with drawstrings
   b. *Northeast*—wooden masks (use papier-mâché) with corn husk hair
   c. *Southwest*—painted or carved cloth or pumpkin masks

• Write a report on mask use today. Point out Mardi Gras costuming and masquerade balls, such as the famous carnival masks made in Ponce, Puerto Rico. Include the use of masks for protection in sports and industry. Show visuals or draw them.

• In the New York/New Jersey area, visit the American Museum of Natural History, and see African and Oceanic masks. In northern New Jersey, visit The

African Art Museum of the SMA Fathers, 25 Bliss Avenue, Tenafly (201-567-0450).
- In New York City, visit El Museo Del Barrio, 1230 Fifth Ave. at 104 St. (212-831-7272) and see their Mexican mask collection.

Activity 27 ============== COME-ALIVE SCARECROWS (1-4)

This enjoyable construction project involves the children in making two-dimensional, movable scarecrows and is suitable for either group or individual activity. It is especially effective when used with children's stories that relate to the scarecrow theme; for example, *The Wizard of Oz* by L. Frank Baum and *Hello, Mr. Scarecrow* by Rob Lewis.

OBJECTIVES

Art
- Create movement in a figure.
- Develop drawing skills with crayons and markers.
- Use cutting, pasting, and assembling skills.

Science
- Understand how bone structure supports the body and how joints facilitate body movement.

History
- Discover how scarecrows have helped farmers in the past and how they help today.

Language Arts
- Develop creative writing skills.

MATERIALS NEEDED

- Covering for desks
- Black and colored markers and crayons
- Fabric scraps
- 2" gummed tape
- Scissors
- Paste and applicators
- White glue
- Dried grass, straw, hay, *OR* shredded paper
- 16 1" brass paper fasteners for each scarecrow
- Chalk

- Pieces of heavy paper in the following sizes for a 4' high figure (sizes may vary):
  one − 6" × 9" (head)
  one − 6" × 9" (hat)
  one − 9" × 12" (torso)
  one − 6" × 9" (hip)
  one − 6" × 6" (joint)
  four − 3" × 9" (arms)
  two − 4½" × 6" (hands)
  four − 3½" × 12" (legs)
  two − 4½" × 9" (feet)

PREPARATION

Make a demonstration model in advance to show the students. Insert the brass paper fasteners at each joint, but complete the figure without any decoration.

DIRECTIONS

1. Introduce the lesson by asking if anyone knows what a scarecrow is and what it is supposed to do. Tell a story about a magical night when a passing star shone on an inanimate scarecrow. The magical star came to help Farmer Brown, whose fields were being cleaned of all new seedlings by hungry birds. Show pictures and other visual materials about scarecrows, and use children's stories that relate to the theme. Discuss the importance of scarecrows to the farmer's newly planted fields.

2. Tell students that this is a special day, because a magical star has empowered each of them to make a scarecrow come alive and help Farmer Brown. Explain that the scarecrow will be constructed in very much the same way their own bodies are constructed. Using students in class and visual materials, discuss how bone structure keeps us supported.

3. Demonstrate how joints work. Show how bodies bend, stretch, turn, etc. Have the entire class stand and practice simple exercises that incorporate body movements and use of joints. Talk about and point to major body joints. Have students do the same. Count each major joint.

4. Using the demonstration model scarecrow, point out the paper fastener at each joint. Show how the joints move. Then discuss how empty the figure is and how it lacks interest. Ask each student for his or her decorating solution. Discuss how clothing parts, pockets, patches, and printed fabric can enliven the figure. Remind students that the figure can be either a man or a woman.

5. Hand out paper for the head and neck. Discuss what kinds of features might be used. Take the chalk and draw the head and facial features. Discuss the drawing and make any necessary changes. Trace over with black crayon or marker. Use other colors for eyes, cheeks, nose, and so on.

6. Hand out paper for the hat. Make one that fits correctly, or, for fun, one that is much too big or much too small.

7. Hand out the torso and hip and joint paper. Decide how to decorate them after the black outlines have been made. Next, hand out arms and legs paper, and follow the same procedure. Use chalk first, make corrections, then color.

 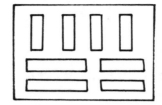

8. Hand out paper for shoes, and follow the same procedures. Students may want to look at the shoes each other is wearing for ideas.

9. Hand out paper for hands. Have students study and draw their hands free-style or trace them. Point out that fingers are a series of joints and cylinders.

10. Review all work at this point. Reinforce good decorating skills. Prepare for the cutting out of segments. Use scissors to cut along the outside edge of the head's black outline. Stress that concentration is needed to cut correctly. Purposely make a mistake, such as cutting off an ear, to illustrate what can happen when attention is not given. Tell the students to begin cutting out all of the body pieces.

11. Discuss the possibilities of further decoration. Suggest the use of fabric scraps for patches, pockets, etc. Glue these in place, using the rubbing paper to ensure good adhesion. Glue or tape the straw or shredded paper to the joints. It should look as if it's coming out of the sleeves.

12. Before assembling the bodies, ask the students to lay out the scarecrow bodies in sequence. Make an intentional mistake, such as attaching a shoe to the head. Wait for the response. In a step-by-step manner, have students place pieces of tape at areas where the fasteners will be used. Push fasteners through the tape and the paper to create movable joints. Start with the head and work down.

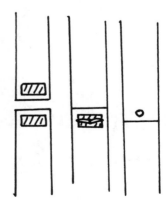

95

13. Arrange the completed scarecrows in an endless array of jointed movements. Hang them from ceiling lights. Attach them to the bulletin board. Hang them from window frames. Ask the students how it feels to have given these scarecrows movement and to have helped Farmer Brown.

FOLLOW-UP

Art
• Have a group of students make a large scarecrow that you can hang from the classroom ceiling.
• Add construction-paper birds (see Activity 40, "Look Up, It's a Plane, It's a Bird, It's a Seagull!") to the scarecrow scenes. Make blackbirds and crows for the scarecrows to "scare" away.
• Repeat system by using Activity 28.

Social Studies
Encourage the students to cut out pictures of major food crops that could be affected by birds. Keep these pictures in a booklet.

Language Arts
• Ask the students to write stories about their own scarecrows and mount them beside their creations.
• Use the scarecrow figures as puppets. Suggest to the students that they write stories with action so that the figures can express the story's activity.

Science
Display the book *The Skeleton Within You* by Philip Balistrino (Harper Junior Books).

Activity 28 ═══════════════════ THE "GO FOR IT" SPORTS FIGURE (3-6)

The coach yells "Go, go, go!" You better have muscles and joints to help make the winning point. These cutout jointed figures help explain how our bodies are divided into

segments and how our joints work. This project serves as good reference material for figure drawing in any picture or construction.

OBJECTIVES

Art
- Improve cutting and assembling skills.
- Observe and copy people in motion.
- Understand size relationships.
- Increase measuring skills.
- Work life size.

Science
- Understand body structure and movement of joints.

MATERIALS NEEDED

- Heavy 80-lb construction paper
- Colored construction paper scraps
- Pencils and erasers
- Scissors
- Tape
- Brass fasteners
- White glue
- Rulers
- Crayons or markers

PREPARATION

To get the students into the spirit of the project, ask them to bring in (ahead of time) pictures of a favorite sports figure in action, in a newspaper, magazine, or on a card, poster, etc. Read "Come-Alive Scarecrows," Activity 27.

DIRECTIONS

1. Demonstrate how joints work. Have the students imitate some of the sports actions. Talk about what is taking place. Show any visuals that illustrate the bone and muscle structures of the body.
2. Draw the figures (see the illustration at the beginning of this activity) on the chalkboard for the students to follow for measurement and shape.
3. Hand out the materials and ask the students to cover their desks.
4. Tell the students to decide whether a straight-on figure or a profile better suits their illustrating a sport movement.
5. Tell the students to begin work on their measuring. They can either measure their body parts or lay on the paper and have their body traced. Check all work before beginning the cutting out.
6. After the measuring and drawing are approved, the students can cut out the segments, lay them out in order, and crayon the uniforms and faces. Assemble the segments with the brass fasteners using the tape as in step 12 of Activity 27, "Come-Alive Scarecrows."
7. Now they can draw the bats, rackets, balls, etc., that the figures will be using. Suggest to the students that they pay attention to the sizes and make

them in relation to the figure. When completed, tape the figures in action around the room.

FOLLOW-UP

Language Arts

Write a short description of what action is taking place, how the bat or ball is being used in relation to the arms, legs, or torso, etc.

Science

Display the book *The Skeleton Within You* by Philip Balistrino (Harper Junior Books).

Activity 29 ================= # SUPER-SIZE WATCH DESIGNS (4-6)

Learn to use flat shapes and color combinations creatively. Everyone wears a watch, so why not design one and get the feel of fashion and industrial design.

OBJECTIVES

Art
* Learn about flat shapes.
* Work with various color combinations.
* Improve cutting and pasting skills.
* Employ imagination and originality in design within an unusual given space.

Math
* Improve measuring skills.
* Learn to compute time differences.

Geography
* Learn about world time zones.

History
* Learn about the evolution of timepieces.

Language Arts
* Improve oral presentations.

MATERIALS NEEDED

* Covering for desks
* Colored construction paper
* Paper punches
* Compasses

- Pencils and erasers
- Heavy white paper for watch faces and display
- Rulers
- Rubbing paper
- Scissors
- Colored crayons or markers
- White glue and applicators
- Brass fasteners
- Oaktag or other heavy paper for watch hands
- Wall world map showing time zones

PREPARATION

Obtain a world map and mark the various time zones. If class time is short, make some circle templates for the students to trace for the watch face. These should have a 6″ diameter.

DIRECTIONS

1. Open the lesson with a class discussion about the importance of time. Ask about getting up on time to catch the school bus, having time to eat, coming in from play, etc. Point to the wall map and explain the world time zones. Ask students to compute the time in various places.
2. Tell the students that they will be designing watches with colored paper and markers or crayons. These won't be watch size; instead, they will be very large, suitable for display. Ask for volunteers to show their watches. Ask them to describe novelty watches they have seen in ads and in stores.
3. Distribute the materials and ask the students to cover their desks.
4. Review circle-making for making the watch face. Demonstrate both freehand and compass-made circles, or use ready-made templates, or use paper plates with cut off rims.
5. Take the white paper and make a circle with a 6″ diameter. Ask the students to make their own circles and mark the center for the placement of watch hands. Now ask the students to use their imagination to design a face for the watch. Let them decide whether or not to include numerals. After the design is completed, cut out the circle.
6. Instruct the students to take a piece of colored construction paper that is larger than the watch face. Place the circle on the paper and measure 1″ away from the face and draw an outline around it. Cut it out and paste the face on it. Cut a small hole at the center mark for the brass fastener.
7. Take oaktag or other heavy paper and draw a pair of hands to fit the face. Measure the radius and use as a guide. Cut out and make a hole for the fastener. Fasten the hands to the face.

8. Take the construction paper and measure two 3½″ × 12″ rectangles for the straps. Each side can be a different color and can have a design. Cut out and take the paper punch and make buckle holes in one of the straps.

9. For the buckle, use a contrasting color. Lay the un-punched strap end on a flat surface and draw the buckle to size. Draw a separate piece for the buckle tongue. Cut out. Paste the buckle and tongue in place.

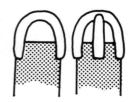

10. Paste the watch on a large sheet of white paper for display.
11. Plan to have each student present his or her watch to the class and talk about its merits, just like a presentation in industry.

FOLLOW-UP

History

Organize a timeline study of the history of keeping time; include visuals and a short presentation of facts.

Activity **30** ================= MY COMIC STRIP (5-6)

Everyone likes the comics, so students will enjoy putting a vacation (or school break) adventure into a comic-strip format. It will be a challenge to present a complete story in three panels, showing a beginning, a middle and an end with accompanying dialogue or commentary.

OBJECTIVES

Art
+ Improve drawing skills.
+ Learn to draw a cartoon strip.
+ Think in sequence.

Language Arts
+ Develop dialogue or story line to fit the pictures.

MATERIALS NEEDED

- Covering for desks
- Pencils and erasers
- Rulers
- Black crayons or markers for outlines
- Colored pencils or markers
- 8½" × 14" white paper
- Paper for story and picture planning

PREPARATION

Tell the students ahead of time to be thinking about a vacation adventure they would like to share with the rest of the class. It will be done in comic strip form. Ask them to bring in comic books and the Sunday newspaper comics section for reference. Also ask them to look at photos taken during the vacation to refresh their memory and give them ideas. To save time, the panel sheets can be photocopied.

DIRECTIONS

1. Ask the students if they have all decided on their story. Ask which are their favorite comic strips and if anyone can name the creator.
2. Direct the students to study the collected strips and to notice that all the drawings have bold black outlines and are filled in with color (like coloring books).
3. Hand out the materials and ask students to cover their desks.
4. Next, ask them to think about how to fit their story into three panels. They can take their extra paper and work on a preliminary sketch.
5. Now the students will take their drawing paper and ruler, and pencil in three 4" square panels, leaving 1" on either side and 2" at top and 2½" at the bottom.
6. Check their measurements before they tackle the drawing.
7. Tell the students to begin the drawings, keeping the outlines simple. When the cartoonists are ready, they can go over the pencil lines with black crayon or marker.
8. Students can add dialogue in the picture or write a story line underneath. Don't forget the title and the cartoonist's name.
9. Now everyone is ready to color the strip. NOTE: If the comics are to be reproduced so that copies can be given to family, friends, *do not color at this time.* Using stencils, spirit masters or copying machines, make copies of the comic strip stories.
10. After copies have been made, color and give them away to friends and family or to the library, principal and school board. This is a different approach to "how I spent my vacation." Save some for classroom display.

FOLLOW-UP

If you live in the New York metropolitan area, visit the Museum of Cartoon Art in Rye Brook, New York (next to Port Chester). Closed on Mondays, the museum is housed in an old mansion.

**MESSAGE ART—DESIGNS
THAT TELL A STORY (3-6)**

Here is a fun project that
shows the impact art has on our
everyday life. These symbols give
directions, express feelings,
identify organizations, religions, or
countries. Students may take
existing message art and add to it
or create their own symbol.

OBJECTIVES

Art
- Become aware of art in everyday life.
- Design a symbol.
- Become acquainted with line and silhouette.
- Increase pencil-coloring skills.

History
- To study the symbolism and design changes of the U.S. flag

MATERIALS NEEDED

- Covering for desks
- Pencils and erasers
- Compasses
- Colored crayons or markers
- Paste and applicators

- 11″ × 14″ white construction paper
- 12″ × 15″ mounting paper in various colors

PREPARATION

Have on hand examples of symbolic art taken from newspapers and magazines. You may need to make some for class reference.

DIRECTIONS

1. Begin the project by showing the design references. Ask if the students see any design symbols in the classroom. Someone will eventually point out the classroom flag. Ask if anyone knows what the stars and stripes stand for. Continue by asking if anyone can relate the story of the designing and making of the first American flag. At this point show the reference material illustrating the flag changes.

Colonial Flags

2. Next, tell the students they will be creating their own art symbols. Show the collected symbols and see if anyone can identify them. Explain what a silhouette is and ask if any silhouettes are shown.

3. Distribute the materials and ask the students to cover their desks. Direct the students to think up their own theme symbols, or design a theme chosen by the class or you. Tell them to begin their outline drawing with pencils.
4. Help anyone who wants to make a circle with a compass.
5. When the penciled design has met the approval of the student, the coloring can begin.
6. After the designs are completed, ask the students to mount the work on colored paper of their choice.
7. Put the work on display and promote a discussion about the designs and their messages.

FOLLOW-UP

Art

The students can create a design that symbolizes their class, showing their interests and aspirations.

History
Have the students copy the design changes in the American flag.

Activity **32** ══════════ # THE HAUNTED HOUSE (2-6)

Here is an entertaining way to introduce watercolor (wash) techniques, or reinforce the lessons of a previous year. Through story telling, lead the class into the assorted terrors of a dangerous swamp, a gloomy forest, and a haunted house. Ask them to provide their own story endings and to paint a picture, illustrating a favorite part of the story.

OBJECTIVES

Art
- Learn the basics of illustration which help to translate a story and a mood.
- Expand compositional skills.
- Explore wash-painting techniques.
- Express a specific mood in a painting.

Language Arts
- To strengthen the use of imagination for story expansion

MATERIALS NEEDED

- Covering for desks
- 16″ × 20″ gray paper
- Water containers
- Palette (small dish or plastic coffee can lid or plastic container)
- Pencils and erasers

- Chalkboard, chalk, erasers
- Paper towels
- Small amounts of black, green, yellow and orange tempera paints)
- #2, #4, #6 and #12 brushes
- 18″ × 22″ black backing paper

For Teacher
- Tapes and/or record player for sound effects
- Candle

PREPARATION

Have tapes or a record player to play eerie mood music and sound effects. Also have a candle to light at certain points of the story. Prepare to lower the shades and dim the lights before telling the following story (or another one of your choosing). It can be a story rooted in fact but it may stray into the unreal—a distinction that many children will soon forget once they are engrossed in the story. Before starting the project, review Activity 4, "Rainbows and Watercolors," to prepare for the painting section of the project.

NOTE

To be effective, this lesson relies upon the ability of the storyteller to weave a tale grounded in some form of reality but that evolves into one of fantasy. It is the movement from what is comfortably real into the unknown that creates the tension and fear appropriate for the session. *A word of caution*—stories for young children in grades 2 and 3 should be tempered so the children do not become too emotionally involved or believe too strongly in the story.

DIRECTIONS

1. Set the tone of the classroom for the tale. Draw the blinds, play appropriate music, and eliminate all possible disruptions (nothing interferes more with a fine story than an unwanted break in concentration and in the build-up of tension and suspense).

2. Introduce the story by mentioning that a class, a group from a prior year, had a scheduled bus trip to the country. Use your name or a colleague's name as the teacher. Name students in the class and (if possible), highlight the name of a student who is no longer attending the school, perhaps someone who changed schools or moved away from the district. Explain that the purpose of the trip was to visit a nearby farm community to do some research on the fall harvest. This community, however, was not accessible from the interstate; instead, it was necessary to travel over some back roads that bordered on a mysterious swamp and forest—a road not often traveled because of the natural elements, but one which cuts time from the trip's length. As the narration progresses, describe the natural features of the area around the road—a dark hemlock forest, the mysterious swamp, paths that lead nowhere; relate stories of hikers who never returned, etc.

3. As the story continues, tell the class that a most unfortunate accident occurred. The bus's front tire became punctured and the bus had to stop. The road was lonely. The only car that came along refused to stop. The bus driver felt he had to get help. He decided to leave the bus in the hands of the teacher and the one parent chaperone, the only other adults on the trip. He would travel back to the main road and try to get some assistance or call the bus company to send another bus. After waiting two hours for the driver to return, the teacher and the parent were becoming very concerned. It was getting dark. No other car had passed this way. No one knew quite what to do.

4. Suddenly, Tommy Brown (the boy who moved away last fall) saw a light in the woods on the other side of the swamp. (Light a candle.) He asked if he

could go and find out whether or not he could get some help there. Reluctantly, the teacher and the parent agreed. Tommy left, followed a path through the swamp, and disappeared into a thicket. An hour passed and Tommy did not return. It was getting darker. The moon was rising and clouds from an approaching storm could be seen racing across its bright luminescent surface. Suddenly a piercing scream came across the swamp. Everyone sat stonefaced and could not move. The question was asked, "Was that Tommy?" No one knew the answer. The light across the swamp flickered. (Blow out the candle.)

5. This time, the parent (use a parent's name) decided she had better go see what had happened. So Mrs. Jones, her son Billy (Mrs. Jones and son might also have moved) and Billy's big friend, Jack, set off across the swamp.

6. Everyone waited and waited for their return. Finally, the teacher and the rest of the class took flashlights and ventured out of the bus and through the swamp. They came upon a mysterious Victorian house with rotting turrets and bays. A light flickered from the top turret window and then went out. They entered the house through its massive oak front door. Once inside, they heard an ear-splitting scream and saw a figure in black on the stairway. (Use any additional ideas from your own imagination). The giant doors closed and the class was trapped inside! Did they escape? Where were their friends? What was that creature?

7. After everyone takes a deep breath, the art lesson can begin. Distribute the paper, paint, brushes, towels, cans of water, palette, etc., to each student or group. (It's suggested that you use groups, since it will be easier to share supplies.)

8. When the students have settled down, review the story and ask the class to solve the mystery. What really happened to all of those people who disappeared? Who was that dark figure on the stairway? Who was screaming? Tell the class that solving the mystery is as important as how well they paint the illustration(s). Tell them to let their imaginations work overtime on this project.

9. At the chalkboard, draw several 16″ × 20″ rectangles, the same size as the paper to be distributed. Encourage the class to discuss the main features or major emotional elements of the story. Make a list: abandoned bus; threatening creature from woods; storm clouds across the face of the moon; bats; owls; a swamp; an immense haunted house with eaves, gables, towers, etc.; large oaken doors; a foyer with covered furniture; a large sweeping staircase; a creature in black floating down the stairs; etc. Ask for several volunteers to come to the chalkboard to draw those images that best cover the story: its beginning, its middle, and its possible solution. When complete, discuss the compositions. Should more trees be added? More clouds? Are there enough bats? Has the creature been defined? Have the students been drawn properly? Do they have enough action? Etc. Ask students to make corrections based on suggestions made from the class.

10. Gather students around a work desk and demonstrate how the painting is to be done. Show them their painting tools. A very fine #2 brush dipped into black paint and water will be used for drawing outlines. Charge the brush with paint and begin roughing out one of the drawings made by the class. Paint as if the brush were a pencil. Pay attention to details. Have the class volunteer suggestions.

11. Change to a larger brush. Add some black to a palette, and add some water to create a wash. With broad sweeping strokes, paint a wash of clouds, the walls of the house, and the gloom of the dark spaces. Work with other size brushes for details: trees, the swamp, etc. Continue using different size brushes with the pigment, making various washes to fill the space and to create a dark mysterious mood. Discuss mood and style as the washes and paintings are worked upon. Continue painting while eliciting suggestions from the class. Let the painting dry a bit. Introduce some other colors. Apply a bit of yellow for the moon, the candle glow, and the flashlight beams. Try some green and orange to accentuate the creature or parts of the house. These are meant to be accents and should not detract from the use of the black paint and washes.

12. After the demonstration, have the students return to their seats and begin their own paintings. Occasionally, stop work and point out good examples being developed. Positive reinforcement always helps, and creates a productive climate. When paintings have dried, mount with the black backing paper and display.

FOLLOW-UP

Art

Find some book illustrations by artists such as Maurice Sendak and Tomi Ungerer who make scary mood illustrations and stories. Display these along with the students' work.

Language Arts

Challenge the students to write a more fully complete *who*, *what*, and *where* of the mystery story, using their own fantasies rather than the answers provided by you. Display these alongside the artwork.

NOTE: With very young children it is important to eliminate the possibility of unanswered questions, such as a missing person, by supplying a suitable answer at the end of the lesson. Older children can play with the possibility of some loose ends. Remember, the story can take on any number of different angles.

Activity 33 ══════════════════ A MEANINGFUL GIFT FOR MOTHER (K-6)

Here's a contribution to the worldwide honoring of Mother during the month of May. Since it was first observed in Philadelphia in 1908, children of the United States have been expressing their love for Mother with gifts on the second Sunday in May. This watercolor painting project for gift giving will illustrate Mother in her various roles in the home, in the workplace, or in the community. This lesson can be used as a reinforcement of watercolor skills or an introduction to the medium. The activity will remind children of the many important and caring things mothers do. It is a very personal gift.

OBJECTIVES

- Introduce or reinforce watercoloring skills.
- Learn composition.
- Learn to observe details and to draw and paint them.

Social Studies
- Gain awareness of and appreciation for mothers' roles.

Language Arts
- Learn to portray events and feelings in words.

MATERIALS NEEDED

- Covering for desks
- Set of transparent watercolor tempera paints
- 11″ × 17″ heavy white drawing paper
- 12″ × 18″ colored backing paper
- Paper towels
- Pencils or fine-line waterproof markers
- #7 brushes
- Coffee can lid palettes
- Containers of water
- Tissues
- Paste and applicators

PREPARATION

Review Activity 4, "Rainbows and Watercolors." Be nonjudgmental on how the subject matter of mother is handled—concentrate on the drawing, composition, and painting technique.

DIRECTIONS

1. Start the lesson with an open discussion about the importance of mothers in our lives, their caring of children and home, and, if employed, the nature of their jobs. Encourage the students to recall events in which their mothers played an important role. (Be sensitive to those children who are being raised by their fathers or other caregivers.)
2. Select several students to draw their story on the chalkboard. Remind them that mother is to be the important figure. Point out that furniture will be smaller than mother, but buildings will be bigger unless in the distance. Further composition study should include large and small objects for variety, large ones balanced by small ones. Details will help explain what is taking place.

3. Have the children discuss the work done on the chalkboard.
4. Group the children in sets of four if possible. Distribute the covering for the desks, drawing paper, pencils or line markers, and ask the students to start work.

5. As drawing progresses, stop the students and hold up examples of full use of picture space and interesting detailing.

6. Ask the students to lay aside their finished drawings while you demonstrate the proper use of watercolors. Have all materials ready. Fill the brush with water and wet the colors in the pans, letting them soften somewhat.

7. Distribute watercolor sets, brushes, water containers, and paper towels. Ask the students to take their drawings and begin adding color to them. Caution students not to get too much water filling their brushes and to wipe excess on the paper towels. Tissues can be used to blot up runny color where not wanted.

8. Stop work and hold up examples that are progressing with good watercolor technique.

9. Let the completed work dry on the desks and ask how the students felt about the colors helping to make a more interesting picture. Mount the dry paintings on the backing paper with paste. Display around the room, and have a discussion about the pictures and how they portray the importance of mothers.

10. Send the pictures home to the mothers just before Mother's Day. Grades 2-6 might include essays.

11. Do the same project for Father's Day.

FOLLOW-UP

Art

Students can make folders large enough to hold the pictures. The stapled folders can act as a gift wrapping and have words and designs to enliven them.

Language Arts

Encourage students to write an essay describing their mother's role in their pictures and try to describe their feelings about it.

Activity 34 ══════════ STORMY WEATHER (3-6)

Use mixed media for different art presentations. The children will use crayons and tempera paint to produce dramatic storm pictures. They will enjoy making magic as they sweep the paint across the picture and see it skid away from the crayoned areas.

OBJECTIVES

Art

* Learn composition, planning, and arrangement.
* Learn the technique of wax resist.
* Learn how to manipulate crayons, brushes, and sponges.

Science
- Study weather systems.
- Understand how climate and tides affect weather.
- Study U.S. coastal erosion problems.

Geography
- Learn map reading.
- Understand the relationship between geography and weather.
- Track storm paths.

Social Studies
- Study a storm's impact on people's lives.

Language Arts
- Use reporting and researching skills.

MATERIALS NEEDED

- Covering for desks
- Pencils and erasers
- Heavy white drawing paper
- Black or dark brown crayons
- Colored crayons
- #10 or #12 brushes
- Sponge pieces

- Containers of water
- Cutdown milk cartons for thinned gray or blue-black tempera paint
- Colored backing paper 1″ larger than drawing paper
- Staplers and staples

PREPARATION

Order audio-visuals and collect photos and news clippings concerning hurricanes and tornadoes. Some *National Geographic* references are: "We're Doing Something About the Weather," (tornadoes), April 1972; "Cajunland, Louisiana's French-Speaking Coast," (hurricanes Audrey, 1957 and Betsy, 1965), March 1966; "Our Changing Atlantic Coastline," (storm erosion), December 1962. Gather examples of storm paintings by such famous artists as Winslow Homer, W. M. Turner, Thomas Cole, Albert Bierstadt and John Stuart Curry. Cut down milk cartons to hold the mixed tempera paint.

DIRECTIONS

1. Introduce the project in a storm season such as early Fall or Spring. Referring to news clippings, magazine photos and weather publications, discuss how storms affect our lives. Ask the students to relate any storm experiences that they or their family may have had.
2. Explain the causes of different kinds of storms like hurricanes and tornadoes. Ask who has seen flooding, buildings destroyed, high surf, soil or sand erosion, and destroyed crops. Talk about acts of heroism and community cooperation in caring for storm victims and the efforts to combat the effects of storms.

3. Ask a student to give a TV-style weather report on a current weather problem. Have the student use a wall map and give reasons for the present conditions.

4. Introduce the subject, a storm picture, by showing slides and other visual materials of the paintings of Winslow Homer, Thomas Cole, W. M. Turner, Albert Bierstadt, Martin Head, and others of the Hudson River School. Also show examples of work by the great midwest artist, John Stuart Curry, who painted dramatic weather settings. Study the composition—the light and dark areas, buildings, trees and other elements of the pictures. Tell the students that their pictures will be made with crayons and paint, known as one form of mixed media.

5. Hand out the materials and ask students to cover their desks.

6. Challenge the students to make a pencil sketch that will illustrate a storm situation. Use the back of the paper for three ideas. Ask the class to discuss the choices.

7. After the choices are made, tell the students to turn the paper over and pencil in the composition they have chosen. Remind them to fill the space well, yet leave enough space for the stormy sky. Stop the class and review the work. Check the size and placement of trees, buildings, people, cars, trucks, animals, etc.

8. Students will now outline the objects in their pictures with a black or dark brown crayon.

9. Ask several students to mix the tempera paint, making a gray with white and black or mixing blue with black. Add enough water so the paint is thin (transparent), called a wash.

10. Demonstrate how the wax crayon will resist the tempera wash. Take some colored crayons and apply them to the paper, pressing and overlapping the colors so that the *wax is dense*. Take a brush or sponge piece filled with paint and lightly pull it across the crayoned areas to show that the paint won't cover the colors.

11. Tell the students to continue to crayon, filling in the outlined objects, pressing down to insure good coverage and using color on top of color for a rich effect. Check the quality of the work before continuing. Paper should not show through in the crayoned areas.

12. Now is the time for all to decide the direction of their storm, which is brought by the wind. A severe storm will appear in a diagonal pattern while a mild rainstorm will appear vertical.

13. Tell the students to apply the paint with either a brush or a sponge. This must be done lightly and not too many times, as the paint can wear away the wax crayon.

14. After the paintings are dry, staple them to backing paper of a contrasting color and display.

FOLLOW-UP

Science, Geography, and Language Arts

• Help develop map-reading skills. Depending on your location, display a wall map of North America or the Pacific Ocean area. Have a volunteer take chalk and mark on the map the paths of major storms of the century. Distribute individual map copies for students to mark. Some major storms of the Eastern United States have been the hurricanes of 1938, 1944, Carol and Diane of 1955, Camille of 1969, and Hugo of 1989. Provide worksheets of storm statistics—size, intensity, damage, etc.

• Prepare students to write reports on storm causes. Tell them to include the role of high- and low-pressure systems, ocean temperature, and the dynamics of upper air streams (jet streams).

• Have students chart the lowest barometer readings in the United States and in their own region. The lowest pressure ever recorded to date was in the Caymen Islands during storm Gilbert in 1988.

• Research major storm target areas in the world such as the typhoon areas of Pacific Asia, Bangladesh, countries bordering the North Sea, the Zeeland flood of the Netherlands in 1953, as well as those affecting the continental United States. Good research references include "Storm Gilbert and the New England Coast" in the September 1988 issue of *Yankee Magazine,* and "The Year the Weather Went Wild" in the December 1977 issue of *National Geographic.*

• Ask students to further increase their research and writing skills by reporting on the subject of the erosion of coastal lands from storms. The problem occurs along the entire eastern coast from Texas to Cape Cod. Even the great salt basin in Utah is affected. New government laws are in effect. Have students tell how the laws will help the situation. A reference on erosion is found in "Our Changing Atlantic Coastline, U.S." in the December 1962 issue of *National Geographic.*

Social Studies

Relate any information on evacuation procedures, temporary shelter, and cleanup operations.

Activity 35 ═══════════════════════════ SNOWY DAY (3-6)

This activity follows Activity 34, "Stormy Weather," and uses the wax resist to produce a snow scene. The students will create an exciting picture of buildings, vehicles, and people in the swirling snow. Get everyone into the feel of the season by reading books such as *Exploring Winter* by Sandra Markle (published by Atheneum).

OBJECTIVES

Art
- Compose a picture with many elements
- Learn the technique of wax resist
- Manipulate crayons and sponges

Social Studies
- Learn about important snowstorms of the past.
- Learn about people's storm experiences.

Science
- Learn the reasons for snowstorms.

Geography
- Track and name locations of arctic storms.

MATERIALS NEEDED

- Covering for desks
- Pencils and erasers
- Black or dark brown crayons
- Colored crayons
- Sponge pieces
- Paper towels
- Containers of water

- White tempera paint
- 11″ × 17″ or 12″ × 18″ or 16″ × 20″ colored construction paper or other heavy paper
- Colored backing paper
- Staplers and staples
- Coffee can lids for palettes

PREPARATION

Collect newspaper accounts of important storms, like those of the Great Plains. Find out how the centennial of the blizzard of 1888 was observed, and research the cold winter in the South in 1983 and 1989, and any others. Assemble as many visuals of snowstorms as possible. Ask the students to bring in any photos they may have of impressive snow scenes. (If you do not live in a snowy region of the country, ask them to bring in magazine pictures.) Collect stories by Jack London and Bret Harte and the poetry of Robert Frost, which describe the impact of winter storms, and read parts of them.

DIRECTIONS

1. Introduce the lesson by telling the students that they will be producing a new weather picture, a snow scene, by using the wax-resist method, as used in their "Stormy Weather" pictures. To create the mood, show all visuals and read the stories and poems about cold winter weather.
2. Tell the students how snowstorms are formed. Ask if anyone knows the difference between a snowstorm and a blizzard. What is a Siberian Express? What is an Alberta Clipper? What does cold air from Canada and warm air from the Gulf of Mexico mean to the United States?

3. Ask a student to take chalk and mark on the wall map the paths that the arctic air masses take. Name which states are most likely to be affected.

4. Talk about storm experiences with impassable roads, stuck cars and trucks, snow removal machines, power outages, school closings, and activities in the snow. If you are living where it doesn't snow, ask the students what they would like to do if they lived in snow country (go skiing, sledding, throw snowballs, build snow forts, etc.). After discussing the events that can happen during and after a snowstorm, tell the students to select an event to use as a picture theme.

5. Hand out the materials and ask the students to cover their desks.

6. Tell the students to sketch several versions of their theme on the back of the paper. Ask the class to make the choice or have the students choose their best sketch and explain the choice. Remind the students to arrange all objects in an interesting manner, yet one which conveys the story. Use a variety of shapes and sizes with the buildings, vehicles, animals, people, trees, telephone poles, snow drifts, and storm clouds.

7. Direct the students to take their paper and turn it over and draw their chosen picture in pencil. When satisfied with the pencil outlines, tell them to go over the lines with a black or dark brown crayon. Add details.

8. Instruct the students to take the colored crayons and apply them to the areas that are to be colored by pressing down and overlapping the colors so that the wax is dense. The color of the background paper should not show through.

9. After the crayoning is completed, tell the students to take a sponge that is *slightly* damp and dip it into the white tempera paint. Remove excess paint on a paper towel. Tell them to think of which direction the wind is blowing and sweep their sponge across the picture accordingly. Add snow to rooftops, tree branches, any surface that the snow would land on or add large snowflakes on top of the wind sweeps or let snowflakes fall gently onto the surfaces. Hold up different pictures that capture the feeling of a windy or a calm snowstorm.

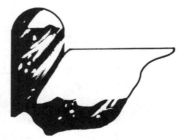

10. When the pictures are dry, staple them to backing paper of a contrasting color and display.

Language Arts

Ask students to write a detailed composition describing what is taking place in their picture.

Science

• Plan a timeline graph showing the amount of snowfall in one region over a period of years.

• Collect data from newspapers, almanacs, and magazines of record snowfalls in the Cascades, Italian avalanches, etc. Mount and put on display.

• Prepare charts that compare snowfall and rain accumulations. Report on why winter snows are important for spring plantings and crops.

• Write to the Commerce Department's Program for Regional Observing and Forecasting Services (in Boulder, Colorado) for information concerning their study on the theory that large star-shaped snowflakes indicate heavy accumulations, while granular flakes frosted with ice indicate a lesser snowfall.

• Write a local TV station, asking how they put on a weather show. Using the information, ask interested students to put on a similar show for the class and explain how it is organized.

Activity 36 ═══════════ SILHOUETTES—VALENTINE KEEPSAKES (K-2)

The perfect memento for parents and/or close relatives is a personalized silhouette. This is an ideal gift that can be framed, become the cover of a book, or be an addition to a family album. Historical references can be made to the late 18th and early 19th century works of both European and American silhouette portrait artists.

OBJECTIVES

Art

♦ Build tracing and cutting skills.
♦ Practice pasting and assembling skills.
♦ Encourage the development of a good self-image.

History

♦ Learn how people in the 18th and 19th centuries recorded likenesses before the birth of photography.

MATERIALS NEEDED

• Covering for desks
• Pencils and erasers
• Fine scissors
• White paste and applicators

• Rubbing paper
• 12″ × 12″ black construction paper

- 14″ × 14″ light background paper
- Tan construction paper
- Darkened room space
- Strong light source (Halogen flashlights)
- Pencils taped to three-foot pointers
- Brown crayons
- Tape

PREPARATION

Have the materials and the special darkened space set up. Working with very young students might require the assistance of a teacher aid or parent helper, at least for the tracing. Some teachers might prefer to do the cutting themselves, while others may let the children work out the problem. Make several silhouettes of objects (apple, cup, shoe, etc.) for demonstration.

DIRECTIONS

1. Introduce the lesson by talking about how images and likenesses were recorded before the advent of photography. Discuss portrait paintings, drawings. Then introduce the subject of silhouettes. Talk about these in general. Have available several examples of silhouettes of various objects, and ask students to identify them. Call attention to detail and introduce the term *profile*.

2. Select a student to pose, and darken the room and/or space. Have the student sit adjacent to a clear wall upon which the sheet of black paper has been taped. To generate more interest, have someone hold the light source while you quickly show some finger shadows (silhouettes on the wall). Turn the light source towards the sitter. Show how the shadow created by the light source can be enlarged or made smaller depending upon the distance from the subject. The ideal distance between subject and light is about five feet, but this has to be determined by you. Once the distance is determined, ask the sitter to sit very still while you 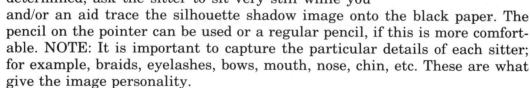 and/or an aid trace the silhouette shadow image onto the black paper. The pencil on the pointer can be used or a regular pencil, if this is more comfortable. NOTE: It is important to capture the particular details of each sitter; for example, braids, eyelashes, bows, mouth, nose, chin, etc. These are what give the image personality.

3. When complete, remove the paper from the wall and begin again. This project does not require a captive audience. Students can be busy at their seats while this activity continues. Here again, the teacher aid or parent can be very helpful. They can do all the tracing work with the very young students. The older students can supervise and assist when difficulties arise. How much adult supervision is required will be determined by you.

4. When the tracing is complete, draw the students' attention to the cutting pro-

cedures. In this particular project, very careful cutting is essential. Use fine scissors. (Original practitioners used cuticle scissors, but any pair of fine scissors will do.) Before cutting on the traced lines, determine if all essential features are in place. Especially important are the eyelashes, a distinctive feature of the face. Have students make corrections if needed. When cutting begins, do not follow the drawn line immediately. It is best to remove excess paper around the image first. Begin by cutting on the neck line and work upward to the hair. NOTE: Instruct and show students that it is easier to cut up into a narrow space and back the scissors out, rather than turn the scissors and risk ripping the paper. This is crucial and should be demonstrated several times.

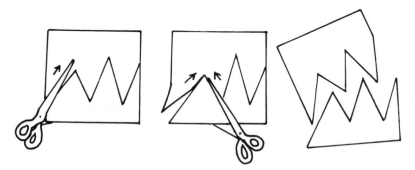

Continue this cutting into a narrow alley and backing out as the cutting proceeds around the shape of the head. Hair ends and decorations should receive special attention. As the eyes are approached, stress the importance of extreme care in cutting this area. Continue exercising the same caution around the rest of the profile.

5. As individual students begin work, check their progress as the cutting proceeds. Stop at intervals and point out areas that require reinforcement. Since exactness is a special requirement of this activity, adult supervision is necessary throughout the tracing and cutting of the image.

6. After cutting, the student can select an appropriate color for the background. White paste is carefully applied to the cleaner side of the silhouette—that side without pencil marks or smudges. The paste should shine and be without lumps. Arrange the silhouette carefully on the background paper, place the rubbing paper on top, and apply pressure. It is completed. At this point, the student should sign his or her name and place the date at the bottom of the project.

7. Other decorative possibilities exist. You might consider doubling the traced paper to make a set of images. These could be used as jackets for a folder or a booklet. Another suggestion is to make a simple frame. After the silhouette has been attached to the background paper, take a tan sheet that is 1¼″ to 2″ larger in both length and width than the silhouette background paper. Trace the silhouette background outline onto the new paper, keeping the margins the same. Remove the silhouette paper. Decorate the exposed margins with crayons or markers to simulate a wooden frame. When complete, fold the margins, including the corners. Apply paste to the back of the silhouette

background paper and attach it within the decorated margins. You now have a silhouette portrait to hang.

FOLLOW-UP

Language Arts

Refer to Activity 2, "I'm Busy Writing a Book." This silhouette project would make an ideal cover for that book project or any other collection of written work by the student.

Art

• Completed works can be displayed in the room on the walls for a special parents night or a back-to-school night. Or, the works could be placed on the students' desks at the same events.

• Present a class guessing game. Cover the names and see who can guess the names by looking at the silhouettes.

Activity 37 ═══════ SILHOUETTES—CITYSCAPES AND SKYLINES (4-6)

Students love this lesson that shows silhouettes of skylines and cityscapes of today or the future. It provides youngsters with the opportunity to observe and consider the architecture of today's great metropolises, and to be aware of the multitude of cityshapes. This lesson can be a good introduction to the study of city life.

118

OBJECTIVES:

Art
- Become familiar with major architectural shapes of city buildings.
- Identify, through silhouette, major architectural forms.
- Build drawing skills that stress detail.
- Explore watercolor transparency as it relates to painting the sky.

Science
- Gain an understanding of the mechanics of sunsets.

Social Studies
- Study life in cities.

Language Arts
- Examine the work of American poets of the early 20th century who wrote about American cities.

MATERIALS NEEDED

- Covering for desks
- Pencils and erasers
- Scissors
- White paste and applicators
- Rubbing paper
- Transparent watercolor setups
- White tempera paint for clouds
- Brushes
- Containers of water
- 12″ × 18″ heavy white paper suitable for watercolor
- 9″ × 18″ black construction paper
- 7″ × 18″ dark gray construction paper
- 13″ × 19″ colored backing paper
- Plastic coffee can lids for palettes
- Paper towels
- Sponges

PREPARATION

Collect and have on hand books and magazines with photographs of American architecture, night scenes of cities, examples of sunsets from American painters of the 19th century, and books on architectural styles. Include a copy of the February 1989 issue of *National Geographic* for the article "Skyscrapers: Above the Crowd." Make at least one building silhouette that is recognizable to most students in the class, such as the Empire State Building in New York City or Big Ben in London. Also have at least one sunset and one silhouette of the neighborhood at the second level (explained in step 8).

DIRECTIONS

1. Hold up the silhouette of a building shape (the recognizable shape suggested) and ask the students to identify it. By questioning the students, see what characteristics enable such identification. Introduce horizontals and verticals. Look for responses that recognize detail and direction of light. Show photographs of city skylines, and ask the students if they would like to try

their hand at developing their own skyline. Show examples of 19th century painters'-use of sunsets and sunrises. Introduce the term *backlighting,* and ask students to determine why this type of lighting best suits recognition of silhouettes. Challenge the students to incorporate both concepts into a project.

2. Distribute the first set of materials: covering for desks, watercolor setups, water, brushes, paper towels, and white paper. Discuss dusk and dawn skies, and observe the paintings of someone such as Martin Heade or Fitz Hugh Lane. Point out the levels of color in sunsets, the richness of the tints and hues, and the blending of many of the edges between the colors. Dampen a piece of watercolor paper with a small sponge after having added several drops of water to each watercolor pan. To a palette, add water and mix several colors—oranges, yellows, blues, reds, and violets. With the damp paper placed on a flat surface, pick up some blues with the brush and apply horizontally across the upper surface of the paper. 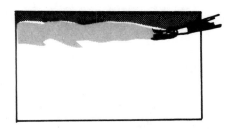 Repeat with the violets, then the reds, oranges, and yellows. Tell the students they can develop their own sequence. As the colors are applied to the damp surface, they will bleed and/or blend together— a desirable quality. If the value or hue is too light, a richer mixture can be reapplied.

3. After the demonstration, try another to reinforce the idea of selection in designing one's own color field. At this point, take another completed example that is dry. Add cloud flourishes by employing a dry brush technique over the completed surface, bringing in brighter colors lower on the page and darker ones near the top of the page. At this point, discuss with the students the atmospheric effects that intrude upon sunsets or sunrises. Ask them what they might consider doing.

4. Now challenge each student to design his or her own sky effect. Check the dampened paper, so that an even amount of water appears. Use a sponge instead of a brush. As work progresses, point out successful and/or unusual effects. When the work is completed, let it dry before attempting special cloud studies. Put the finished work aside for the next stage.

5. Show how a silhouette can be made from a piece of black paper by drawing the image in pencil and very carefully cutting it out. Ask students the kinds of silhouette images that they might like to incorporate into their skylines. Stress variety, individuality, uniqueness, etc. Distribute black paper and pencils. Challenge the students to draw their own skylines, choosing those that exist today or those that might exist in the future. Stress the concept that many structures that exist today will also intermingle with those that come tomorrow! Using slides, prints, and/or photographs, present a brief survey of the development of the American skyscraper and architecture in general. This silhouette will show the tallest buildings in the activity.

6. As drawing progresses, occasionally stop to reinforce good examples. Stress those that include special details, such as church spires, water tanks on top of apartment buildings, the unique tops of Art Deco buildings of the 1930's, and

the resurgence of these ideas in the 1980's—not to mention the international modernist styles of the 1950's, 1960's and 1970's. If mistakes are made, have students erase them. The students must *not* turn the paper over to begin again. *One clean, unmarred side is needed.* Continue observing and commenting about the work until skylines are completed.

7. Review the cutting procedures. It is easier to cut up into a narrow space and back out rather than turn the scissors. Stress the importance of keeping as much detail as possible intact. Cut out the complete skyline and put it aside.

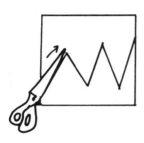  

8. Discuss the second level of a skyline. The second level refers to buildings in the outskirts of the city, the neighborhoods with school buildings, homes, churches, synagogues, etc. Show examples made. Reinforce with photographs that illustrate both the high central city skyline the second level lower skyline. Ask students about the features that are characteristic of the second level. Ask what  they might like to consider putting in theirs. Distribute dark gray paper and challenge them to create their own local neighborhood skyline. Stress attention to detail, and underline the concept of scale. The scale of the neighborhood skyline will be one of low verticals. It will be more horizontal in feeling. As work continues, reinforce good examples. When completed, check for errors, correct them, and then cut out.

9. At this point, a third level might be considered for those who wish to do so. This level would include those shapes that appear on the outskirts of cities such as airports, ships, shipping terminals, highway approaches, bridges, etc. Including the third level would expand the project to a higher level, but is certainly within the ability ranges of students in grades 4-6. The color selected might be another gray or black.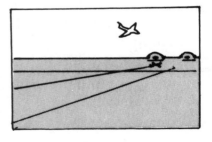

10. When the two or three silhouetted skylines have been completed, arrange them on the dry surface of the watercolored sky with the most distant silhouette to be placed first on the page followed by the others in sequence. Arrange the spacing between each for the best effect. (If three levels are used, the last

might include silhouettes cut along the bottom edge. This would suggest the reflection of the sky in water which can create a dramatic effect.)

11. After the arrangement has been decided upon, lightly pencil to mark placement and remove the silhouettes. Carefully apply a thin coating of paste to the entire back surface that has the pencil marks and smudges. Place on the watercolor. Adjust. Apply the rubbing paper and press. Repeat with the other levels or silhouettes. When finished, apply a contrasting color backing paper and display.

FOLLOW-UP

Language Arts
• Display the silhouettes along with written reports describing the buildings and their uses.
• Read and discuss the poems of 20th-century poets who wrote about American city life. Copy a favorite poem or stanza, and display it with the artwork. You might use the work of Walt Whitman and Carl Sandburg.

Science
Discuss the mechanics of sunrises and sunsets.

Activity 38 ══════ HANGING VALENTINES (1-5)

Midwinter is time for love and remembrance. Simple, decorated, and personalized valentines are wonderful gifts for family members and other special people.

OBJECTIVES

Art
♦ Learn how to measure shapes.
♦ Increase tracing skills.
♦ Use cutting, pasting, and assembling skills.

History
♦ Become familiar with heart shapes used in various cultures in past times.

Language Arts
♦ Become familiar with poetry and sayings appropriate for valentines.

MATERIALS NEEDED

• Covering for desks
• Pencils and erasers
• Scissors
• White paste and applicators

• Rubbing paper
• Colored cotton roving in reds, whites, silvers, pinks, magentas, etc.

- Writing paper to fit heart shapes
- Colored construction paper in red, white, pink, magenta, etc.
- Doilies

- Instant cameras and film OR colored markers, 8½″ × 11″ white vellum paper, and hand mirrors

PREPARATION

Have a demonstration model ready but not yet assembled. You'll need several heart shapes of different sizes, lengths of cotton roving, cut-off edges of doilies, photographs, selections of poetry, drawn portraits, etc. Gather illustrations of folk art heart designs and fancy old-fashioned valentines. Set up a work space with lighting if instant camera pictures are to be taken.

DIRECTIONS

1. Use historical examples from art texts—folk heart motifs of Germany, Austria, Hungary, and German Pennsylvania Dutch origin; American valentines of the Victorian and early 20th century; and poetry and verse of Romantic England during the 19th century. Introduce the role of valentines in our culture. Ask students to recall their use within that special context. Keep the conversation flowing with positive and romantic images of the holiday remembrance.

2. Challenge students to think about creating a special token for a family member, or other special person, using the concept that the most personal memento is something you make yourself to give to another. It is even more personal if it includes an image of the giver. Ask students how this can best be accomplished. Demonstrate the use of the instant camera as a means of capturing an image *or* rely upon a mirror to help copy the student's image, using markers or colored pencils. Either method can be as meaningful as the other. Point out that miniature portraits painted on ivory were given as gifts before the invention of the camera.

3. Begin the process by establishing the variety of valentine heart shapes. Some are long, others are tiny, while still others are particular to a special region, like those of the Pennsylvania Dutch. By taking a very large piece of paper and folding it in half, demonstrate how you can make a perfectly balanced valentine shape by drawing only one half of the image along the folded side. Using a pair of scissors, cut out the folded shape. Ask a student to repeat this procedure by designing his or her own type of heart and cutting it out. To illustrate the importance of the fold, purposely make a mistake and draw the image along the open side. Ask a student to cut it out to see that the result is a pair of half hearts.

4. Reinforce the importance of individually designed heart shapes by having several students develop their own. Use tape and attach the hearts to the chalkboard. Have a discussion on how these compare with the historical examples.

5. Select the image-making process. The instant camera shot will measure about 3¼″ × 4¼″, while the drawing can be larger. Demonstrate the opera-

tion of the instant camera. Use the space with lighting and background appropriate for taking a photo. You should help younger students with this work; older students can be taught to operate the camera, using a team approach. Put the photos aside. The drawings should be made with the help of a hand mirror, so that each student can refresh his or her memory as to how he or she looks. Using the markers and/or pencils, students should do a rather detailed self-portrait, concentrating on the head. Stress special individual characteristics, such as cowlicks, freckles, eyeglasses, eye and hair colors, etc. Put the completed drawings aside.

6. Hand out the paper for the first series of valentines. Each student should receive two sheets of paper that are the same size. These should be big enough to incorporate the image from the drawing or photo. Fold one piece of paper in half. Along the folded edge, have students *draw half* a valentine heart shape. Cut out the first shape.

7. Take the shape and trace it onto a second sheet of paper to obtain an exact replica. Cut it out.

8. Trim the photo or drawing to fit on the heart shape. Another idea is to cut out a heart shape frame in a different color to place over the picture. Follow the original edge, but measure ½", or so, inward. Cut it out, paste the picture onto the first heart and place the frame over it.

Frame   Backing

9. Now challenge the students to decorate the entire edge of the valentine. Small hearts can be cut out and pasted on the edge, as can the doily edging. The possibilities are endless. Ask the students for suggestions. When the first heart is completed, hand out writing paper and more construction paper. Find some appropriate saying, or have the students carefully write their own, original sentiment. On a sheet of lined or plain paper, cut a heart shape, somewhat smaller than the original heart, and write the sentiment. This can be pasted to the original shape, but can also be decorated, using the markers or pencils, with flowers or small hearts interspersed with the written sentiment.

10. When both sides of the first heart have been completed, take the length of colored roving and place it on the desk surface. Determine how many hearts may be used in the hanging and where the major heart shape will be placed. Cut them out as before. Carefully apply white paste to the back of the first heart. Place the front side down on a desk. Align the roving along the heart's center (from top divide to pointed end). Place the second heart in place exactly on top of the first heart, and apply pressure. This will create a double-sided heart, through which a colored piece of roving runs.

11. Now challenge the students to design as many other double-sided hearts as they can to be run above and below the one just completed. Other hearts may incorporate sayings, as well as the names of the person or persons to whom the valentine will be given. The original hanging can have as few as four or as many as eight to ten hearts along the roving. A small heart should end the bottom. The roving can be knotted at the top for easy hanging.

FOLLOW-UP

Art

All heart hangings can be displayed in the classroom prior to their being taken home or sent to that special person.

Language Arts

The written sentiment can form the major part of this lesson, with emphasis on the development of the written message. If the message is written as poetry, you might want to teach the writing of a quatrain.

Activity 39 ═══════════ COME OUT, COME OUT, WHEREVER YOU ARE! (4-6)

Color, line, and shape, used in mixed media, are the ingredients in this composition. Students will draw animals in a setting that will hide them from easy detection (camouflage). The picture can be realistic in style or purely imaginative.

OBJECTIVES

Art
- Use previous knowledge of line, shape, and color.
- Experience working in mixed media.

Science
- Learn how animals use camouflage for protection.

125

Language Arts
- ✦ Write a report on some aspect of animal camouflage.

MATERIALS NEEDED

- Covering for desks
- Markers and crayons
- Tempera paints
- 16″ × 20″ gray paper
- Heavy white paper, if a snow scene
- Coffee can lid palettes

- Pencils and erasers
- Containers of water
- #2, #4, #6, and #12 brushes
- 18″ × 22″ black backing paper
- Paper towels
- Paste and applicators

PREPARATION

Display as many visual references as possible of mammals, insects, birds, and fish in their native habitat. Some reference material on animal camouflage can be found in the following publications: *How Animals Hide* (a National Geographic children's book, 1973); *Find the Hidden Insect* by Joanna Cole and Jerome Wexler (Morrow); "Tracing the Snow Leopard" in the June 1986 issue of *National Geographic;* and "Scorpion Fish: Danger in Disguise" in the November 1987 issue of *National Geographic.* Have reference material available before the project time to enable the students to make their animal choices and to be ready to go to their work quickly.

DIRECTIONS

1. Distribute the materials and ask students to cover their desks.
2. Review the use of colors.
3. Ask if anyone has made their animal choice. Encourage the students to use most of the following materials—paints, crayons, markers and/or pencil—in one composition. They will be using what artists call mixed media.
4. Circulate around the workspace and offer help when needed. Guide the children to try and be as clever as the animals in choosing a camouflage design. Make animal design work with background color, plants, rocks, flowers, trees, etc.
5. After the work is completed and dry, ask the students to mount it on the backing paper. Have a contest to find the hidden animals in the project display.

FOLLOW-UP

Science and Language Arts
Assign an essay-writing lesson describing the food-gathering, care-of-young, and survival techniques of the animals in the project.

Activity **40** ════════════ **LOOK UP, IT'S A PLANE, IT'S A BIRD, IT'S A SEA GULL! (3-6)**

This activity brings the outdoors into the classroom. The children will be involved in a project that can have exciting results. They will construct realistic-looking paper sea gulls that can soar over their heads from the lighting fixtures. This is a creative way to celebrate National Bird Day on April 10. Follow this activity by painting a mural background for the birds. (See Activity 41.)

OBJECTIVES

Art
- Use observational skills.
- Learn to work in dimension.
- Study proportion.
- Use cutting and pasting skills.

Science
- Understand the interdependence of birds, fish, and plants.
- Study bird feeding and nesting styles.
- Study flight patterns and migrations.

Social Studies
- Study the need for protected areas.

Language Arts
- Write reports and essays.

Geography
- Locate coastal boundaries and national shoreline parks.

MATERIALS NEEDED

- Covering for desks
- Pencils and erasers
- Scissors
- 9″ × 12″ (gulls) and 9″ × 6″ (smaller birds) construction paper in various colors and white

- Paste and applicators
- Rubbing paper
- Black markers
- Paper punches
- Scrap paper in gray, gold, yellow, and black for details
- String

PREPARATION

Make a sample paper-gull construction, following steps 7 through 17, for reference. Order audio-visual materials and collect as many pictures of coastal birds in their native habitat as possible. *National Geographic* references are: "Can We Save Our Salt Marshes?" (June 1972); "The Imperiled Everglades" (January 1972); "Life in a 'Dead Sea': Great Salt Lake" (August 1967); "The World and How We Abuse It" (December 1970); "The Triumphant Trumpeter Swan" (October 1985); "Duck Hunting With a Color Camera" (October 1951); and "Saving Man's Wildlife Heritage—Audubon Sanctuaries" (November 1985).

DIRECTIONS

1. Tell the students that this and the following activity involve the study of birds living along the coasts and wetlands of the U.S. They will make realistic-looking paper sea gulls that will be "flying" in the classroom.
2. Show all the visuals of gulls, terns, etc., and their coastal and inland sea homes. When showing films, encourage close attention to the body shapes and construction, flight patterns, and the beauty of the soaring birds.
3. Ask a student to trace the coastal boundaries of all fifty states on a wall map. These will include river boundaries.
4. Invite a class discussion about the interrelationship of birds, aquatic animals, land animals, and their need for food. Include visuals of various shore rock formations, sandy shores and marshland. List types of vegetation on the chalkboard. Continue the study using visuals of nesting styles and migration paths.
5. Ask students to locate the following National Shoreline Parks on a map: Acadia National Park, Maine; Barneget National Wildlife Refuge, New Jersey; Cape Cod National Seashore, Massachusetts; Cape Hatteras National Seashore, North Carolina; Cape Lookout National Seashore, North Carolina; Everglades National Park, Florida; Gateway National Recreation Park, New York; Hawaiian Islands National Wildlife Refuge; National Lakeshore Park Picture Rocks, Michigan; Olympic National Park (coast), Washington; Padre Island, National Island Park, Texas; Point Reyes National Seashore, California; Sleeping Bear National Lakeside Park, Michigan. There is also a way station of protected land for migrating birds in the New Jersey/Delaware area called Reed's Beach, on Delaware Bay. Ask students why these and local areas need protection for wildlife.
6. Hand out the materials and ask the students to cover their desks.
7. Tell the students to select a 9″ × 12″ gray or white paper for the gull's body and fold it in half the long way.

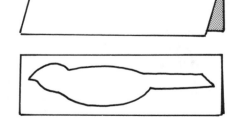

8. Refer to the sample gull before sketching the body. Tell everyone to study the proportions carefully and then sketch the body lightly in pencil, filling the entire length of the paper. Check the head and tail sizes with the sample. Make corrections and complete drawing.

9. Cut out the gull body. There will be two pieces.

10. Apply a thin layer of paste to the one piece with the pencil lines. Fit other piece on top of it and align. Place rubbing paper on top and apply pressure with hand, assuring good adhesion.

11. Take a piece of gold paper and fold it in half. Place the bird's body on top and trace the beak outline onto the gold paper. Cut out and paste beak sides onto the bird body. Draw and cut out gold-colored legs showing the flying position and paste in place.

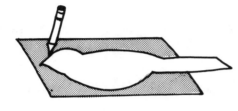
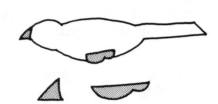

12. Take a black marker and draw the eyes, black markings on head and on feet or use pieces of black paper instead.

13. For the wings, take a piece of 18″ × 6″ white paper and fold it the long way. Draw a wing shape and cut it out. Also cut out and paste gray feather pieces onto the wings of young adult gulls. Erase nonessential pencil lines.

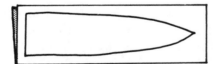

14. Hold the body in place and determine wing placement. Caution the students to leave enough room between the top of the gull's back and the bend of the wing for a hole for string. Holding the wing tips pointing up, decide on placement and mark with a pencil at the bottom of the wing.

15. Apply paste to the top side of the straight edge of the wing and paste where indicated. Flip the gull over and do the same on the other side.

16. After the wings are set, take the paper punch and make a hole about halfway between the width of the wings. Check for the center of gravity.

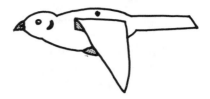

17. Attach string and hang from light fixtures. Encourage the students to make smaller shore birds—sandpipers, snipes, and ducks—from the 9″ × 6″ pieces of paper. Some should have one flat side for placement on the mural. (See Activity 41.)

FOLLOW-UP

Language Arts

Explain the difference between writing a report and writing an essay. (See the following follow-up activities.)

Science

Have the students write a report on "How do weather changes influence the behavior of coastal birds?"

Social Studies

• Have the students write a report on "Why is the sea gull the state bird of Utah?"
• Essay topics might be: "If I were a sea gull for a day, I would . . ." (be at garbage dumps looking for food, dropping shellfish dinners onto the sand or parking lots, etc.); and "How I would help promote interest in protecting a natural local area."

References

The following resources are helpful: *Coastal Rescue—Preserving Our Seashores* by Christina G. Miller and Louise Berry (Atheneum); *Birds* by Herbert S. Zim and Ira N. Gabrielson (Golden Press); and *The Birds Around Us* (Ortho Books, Chevron Chemical Co., Consumer Products Division, 575 Market Street, San Francisco, CA 94105).

Activity 41 ================= OUR OWN SEASHORE MURAL (3-6)

In this activity, the children will be challenged to create an environment for the gulls and other birds created in Activity 40. They will experience group cooperation in planning and painting a mural. The flying gulls and the mural make an impressive display. The students will be eager for others to view it.

OBJECTIVES

Art

- ◆ Sketch a large area.
- ◆ Paint a large area.
- ◆ Combine different paper objects in one composition.
- ◆ Use natural objects for added interest.

MATERIALS NEEDED

- Covering (newspaper or drop-cloth) for floor
- Covering for desks
- Brown kraft paper cut to mural size
- Tempera paints
- Cutdown milk cartons
- Water containers
- Paper birds from Activity 40
- #4, #6 and #10 brushes
- Sponges, rags and sticks
- Chalk
- Tall grass or cut paper to look like grass
- Masking tape
- Paste and applicators
- Paper towels

PREPARATION

Collect newspapers or obtain plastic dropcloths for covering the floor. Cut down milk cartons for mixed colors. Ask the students to collect tall grasses to paste onto the mural. Review color mixing and landscape painting. (See Activities 4 and 19.) Allow time for paint-drying periods. Collect visuals of shore scenes.

DIRECTIONS

1. Ask the students to lay floor coverings and to cover their desks.
2. Show visuals of coastal scenes—marshlands, beaches, or rocks. Involve several students in sketching a scene on the chalkboard. Invite class discussion about the work.

3. Hand out the rest of the materials.
4. Select groups of students to chalk-sketch the basic composition of sky, land, water, and plants on the kraft paper. Remind them to fill the surface with sweeping, free design, using the visual resources for reference. Another group of students can give their opinions and offer suggestions for changes or additions.
5. Review color mixing. (See Activity 4.) Ask students how to obtain orange, brown, or blue-green. Review landscape painting. (See Activity 20.)
6. As a time saving measure, consider pre-mixing colors.
7. Choose groups to paint in different areas. Direct a group to begin on the ground area and continue on to the water. All the painting should be applied with free, broad brush strokes and sponges and rags for varying effects. NOTE: Too much paint on the applicator can cause problems. It is better to add more paint with the next application than risk water damage to the paper.
8. Let each area dry before continuing. This may require a day to happen, so the project covers more than the usual time span.
9. Ask a group to paint the clouds and grasses and other plants. Use semi-moist sponges for the clouds. Use #6 and #10 brushes in a dry-brush technique for rendering the grasses, etc. For speckled sand, dip a dry brush into thick paint and move it up and down rapidly, lightly touching the paper. Also use sticks for the same effect. Add white reflections on the water. IMPORTANT: All previous work must be dry!

10. When completed, let the mural dry in an out-of-the-way place. Then attach it firmly on a wall or large bulletin board for further work.
11. Tell the children to collect the birds made in the previous activity and plan where to place them on the mural. Have the birds feeding, sitting on eggs, feeding the young, seeking food, etc.
12. Arrange the birds and use masking tape to hold them in place.
13. Mark placements in chalk. Remove tape from the birds and paste them in place using rubbing paper to insure good adhesion.
14. Paste the gathered grass on the mural. Cut paper grasses of green and tan paper if real grass cannot be found. Cut them in varying lengths and shapes as marsh grasses grow in many varities. Let some of the grass hide part of the birds for an added touch of realism.

15. Hang the gulls from the previous activity in a flight pattern near the mural.
16. Upon completion, invite other classes and parents to view the display. Don't forget to take photos!

Just what we need to enhance an interstellar or planetary space mural—a fleet of space machines suspended in air! This project not only reviews and reinforces concepts of mathematical volumes, it also neatly uses recyclable materials.

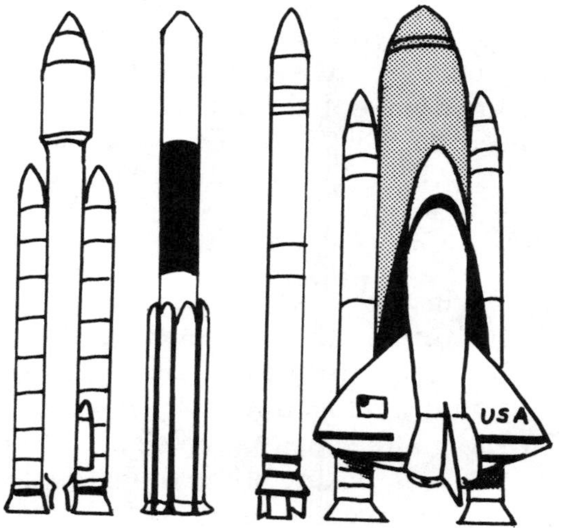

Titan III   Delta II   Atlas   Columbia Shuttle

OBJECTIVES

Art

* Assemble found volume-objects into thematic forms.
* Use a variety of materials to enhance these forms.

Math

* Review and reinforce mathematical concepts relating to volumes.

Science

* Use contemporary research on space travel for the construction of the space vehicles.

History

* Gain an understanding of the development of rocketry from its inception in the United States, the Soviet Union and Germany to today's products.

MATERIALS NEEDED

* Covering for desks
* White glue
* Rubbing paper
* Scissors and cutting knives (CAUTION: To be used under adult supervision)
* Metallic spray paint and spray booth
* Tempera paint
* Metal foil and aluminium
* Plastic pill containers with lids
* Square scraps of railroad board, silver if possible
* Assorted plastic containers
* Assorted cardboard cylinders (paper towels, toilet tissue, adding machine paper, rug tubes)
* Assorted pieces of cardboard or mat board
* Heavy railroad board
* Craft sticks, tongue depressors, toothpicks
* White or black thread
* Dishwashing liquid for painting on plastic coating
* Large toothpaste boxes
* Red, white, blue, and silver tapes
* Coffee can lids
* Compasses and rulers

PREPARATION

Have a selection of space books available that relate to space travel rocketry. Show illustrations of past and current vehicles for space travel, as well as artists' conceptions of how they might look in the future. (See "Columbia" in October 1981 issue of *National Geographic*.) Gather some of the paper cylinders and materials and begin to assemble a space traveler. Two options are available: Use current knowledge and information on space travel OR imagine space travel of the future (like *Star Wars*). Challenge the students to work *in either direction*.

DIRECTIONS

1. Begin the project by exploring the theme options. Draw upon models and illustrations that currently exist. Notice that most configurations today look like several cylinders tied together. These contain various kinds of fuel cells, liquid hydrogen and/or solid fuel discs. Atop this or attached to it would be the manned space vehicle, which can look like the shuttle, the Apollo moon vehicles, or any other vehicles used by the U.S., the Soviet Union, or the European Space Agency. Select different sized cylinders. On class-made cylinders close the ends off with either cones or circles with tabs. (See Activity 13.) This time, use the heavier railroad board.

2. Hand out the materials and ask the students to cover their work spaces.

3. Review use of the compass. Take a square of the railroad board that will be large enough in size to cover the end of the cylinder. Three 4″ squares should suffice. Draw the circle. Cut it out and make a cut equal to the radius. Overlap these cuts to make a cone.

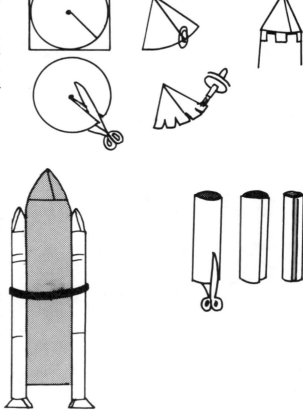

Increase the overlap until the correct-size cone is made. Glue the overlap, and add a paper clip until it sets. Cut the tabs to fit inside the cylinder. Use white glue and an overnight set to hold firmly in place. Make other cones to suggest thrusters at the opposite end. Bind these together with a rubber band *after* the manned vehicle is designed. Cardboard paper towel cylinders can be made narrower by cutting, rolling, and taping.

4. The manned vehicle can consist of boxes, cylinders, pill containers, flat cardboard shapes, etc. Groups of these can be bound together, and then fins can be added by scoring and bending the cardboard. To score, take the fin shapes and use a ruler and a sharp edge to make a line that cuts into the cardboard by about one-half of its thickness. Make a fold in the opposite direction. This creates an edge and surface which can be glued to another surface.

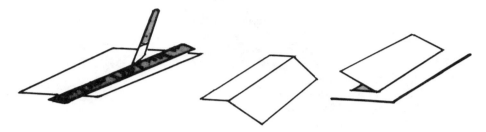

Challenge the students to assemble their own vehicles, based on illustrations. Have them use craft sticks, toothpicks, etc. Glue pieces together and let dry. In this instance, it is better to let the creative ability of each student solve the problem. As work is being done, make sure manned vehicles are in scale and can be attached to the booster rockets. Use rubber bands, clips, paper tabs, or glue.

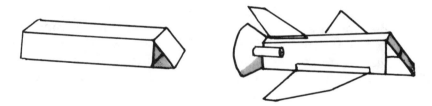

5. When dry, use a spray booth or work outside to spray both the liftoff and the manned vehicles with a silver spray paint. CAUTION: Use correct safety precautions to do this! Masks, goggles, etc. should be used. Let dry. If painting instead with tempera paint, mix four parts paint to one part dishwashing liquid for painting plastic-coated surfaces.

6. After the paint has dried, have students use foil, colored tapes, and insignia found from different sources to add details to both the liftoff vehicles and the manned spacecraft. Use white glue again. If students want to add personal

touches, they can add details using fine-line permanent markers.

7. Using the pointed end of a compass, make two holes in the main craft. Thread string through both, tie off on open paper clips, and hang from the

light fixtures in the room. You now have a manned space flight in operation!

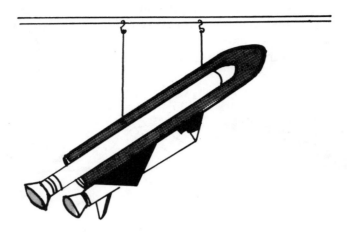

DIRECTIONS FOR STARSHIPS

Rather than opting to mimic contemporary space vehicles, challenge the students to use their imagination to design their own, for space travel in the future. Turn to the illustrations used in such films as the *Star Wars'* trilogy, *Alien, Star Trek* movies, etc., and the wealth of ship design that has been created—starships, battlestars, overdrive vehicles, etc. Use all available materials mentioned before but do not impede students' imagination. The sequence for joining the volumes and flat shapes together remains the same. Take individual pieces, such as cylinders, and then make the components. Glue together and dry overnight before painting. This time, all kinds of colors can be used. Let paint dry overnight and then add details, plastics, insignia, etc.

DIRECTIONS FOR THE SPACE STATION

Make an exciting project with all available materials. Have students work in groups to design a space station. Model it after the Soviet Union's Soyuz Station, or after the form first seen in the film *2001, A Space Odyssey,* or make an imaginary station.

FOLLOW-UP

Art

Supplement the work on the space vehicles by designing those that have been used in the last thirty years. Start with the Sputnik and move on to the Viking and the Discovery series. Use found and made materials. These forms, which are generally smaller, can be added between the space craft.

Language Arts and History

• This project alone has enough material for a series of reports, written articles, and/or journalistic events. One group might prepare a history of rocketry, another the history of American/Soviet space exploits, another information gleaned from the probes sent to nearby planets. Other groups might like to invent a journalistic survey of what might occur when the first astronaut steps foot on Mars or on a satellite of Jupiter. The possibilities are endless.

• Follow the spacecraft flight listed below and construct art projects and written information to accompany each:

—*October 1989,* launching of Galileo for a rendezvous with Jupiter in 1995
—*April 1990,* launching of the Hubble Space Telescope
—*August 1990,* Magellan mission began orbiting Venus
—*1992,* launching of Mar's Observer
—*1995,* proposed launching of Comet Rendezvous Asteroid Flyby mission
—*1996,* proposed launching of Cassini mission to orbit Saturn in 2002

Science

If possible, visit the Air and Space Museum in Washington, D.C.

References

More information can be obtained in *Spacecraft* by Robin Kerrod, with a pull-out poster (Random House), and "Columbia Closes a Circle" in the October 1981 issue of *National Geographic.*

Activity 43 ============ GIANT STUFFED FISH OR WHALES (3-6)

This exciting project can be an unrelated lesson or the perfect complement to a mural painting lesson depicting undersea life. These giant-sized stuffed fish or whales present a sensational-looking sea environment right in the classroom.

OBJECTIVES

Art

♦ Explore volumes in real-life forms.
♦ Develop lifelike and close to life-size shapes of known forms.
♦ Explore the arranging of objects in a three-dimensional space.

Science
  - Learn about the different sea species of fish and mammals.

Math
  - Refine measuring skills with respect to sea life measurements.

Language Arts
  - Use art, math, or science as a base for writing reports, essays, or stories about sea life.

MATERIALS NEEDED

  - Covering for desks and/or floor
  - White chalk
  - Double sheets of kraft paper in differing sizes
  - 9″ × 12″ newsprint for sketches
  - Pencils and erasers
  - Tempera paints in various colors
  - #4 and #7 brushes in 2″, 3″ 4″ widths (bristle or sponge types)
  - Scissors
  - Staplers and/or white glue
  - Newspaper for floors and a larger supply for the fish
  - Markers
  - String, large paper clips, or paper clamps
  - Green construction paper
  - White paste and applicators
  - Containers of water
  - Masking tape

PREPARATION

First, make a small demonstration model out of the kraft paper, with a string attached to hang from the light fixture. Gather, or set aside in the school library, an array of research materials such as books, film strips, films, videos, posters, prints, etc. Have a flashlight available.

DIRECTIONS

1. Stimulate the students to want to further decorate their room or hallway space after they finish painting an undersea mural, or suggest they do it as a separate project. Ask them how they would make the room appear like an undersea environment. Turn off the classroom lights. Turn on the flashlight and cast the light about the room. Tell the students to imagine that this room is in the sea. Let the light fall upon the one completed fish. Ask the students to imagine the entire room filled with a variety of sizes and species. Ask them if they would like to make monster-sized sea creatures like whales and sharks.
2. After the energy and enthusiasm have been generated, demonstrate how this can be done. The project can be done by individual students or as a group. If large fish/whales are attempted, it is best to do group work. Using slides, posters, prints, television tapes, etc., cover the field of underwater sea life. Stress the region and species to be considered. For example, cover fish life of the North Atlantic, the Gulf of Mexico, or the Pacific Northwest. Or the subject might be endangered whales, or the sharks of the Great Barrier Reef off

Australia. Whatever the choice, use the slides and audio-visual materials as the resource base. Oversee individual and/or group research.

3. When choices and research have been completed, hand out newsprint and pencils, paper clips and scissors and ask the students to rough out their sketches of the fish before using the kraft paper. Refer to the resources to correct drawings, making them as lifelike as possible. Ask the students not to make exact copies of the source material. Each student should render the fish accurately, yet show his or her individuality.

4. Select the size of kraft paper appropriate to form the fish or whale. Take two sheets and clip both sheets together, placing clips at intervals around the edges of the paper. With chalk, outline the fish or whale selected. Refer to the original sketch. Make 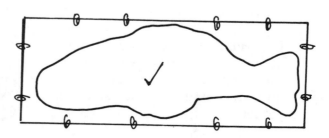 corrections. Make sure the space is filled and the outline details are included. Cut out the image along the chalk lines. Move the clips to new positions as cutting proceeds, so that both sheets keep their exact shapes. After cutting is done, mark the outsides, as these are the sides to be painted. (NOTE: Review and reinforce proper cutting procedures before cutting begins and while it is being done.)

5. Hand out the remaining materials and cover the work spaces. Prepare the paints. Mix colors in coffee cans or plastic containers. The fish or whales have general colors and then areas requiring other shapes, tones, or tints. Place newspapers on the floor. Place one side  of the cutout fish or whale face up on the newspaper. Using large 2″ or 3″ brushes or sponge brushes, apply a coat of paint to the top surface. Blend lighter or darker colors for such areas as the bellies and darker shades for the upper areas. When complete, allow to dry. Then move the dried work to a safe place and repeat with the other side. Be sure it matches up with the completed side. Allow to dry.

6. Return to the first side. Add details using other paint colors or markers. Refer to major sources and to drawings. Consider barnacles on whales, skin texture on sharks, scales and colorings on fish. Do careful work on eyes, teeth, mouths, gill areas, and especially the fins (dorsal, anal, gill, etc.). Allow to dry. Do the other side. Make sure that the eyes are exactly opposite each other.

7. Consider other details that might be needed. Gill fins will have to be made and attached to each side. Take two pieces of paper, paint details on both sides, and attach to the body through a cut slit in the body section. Be sure to mark for the slit in the correct position.

8. When both sides have been completed, apply white glue to the edges around 7/8 of the fish—*leave the mouth area open.* Place the companion piece on top, making sure that they are perfectly aligned.

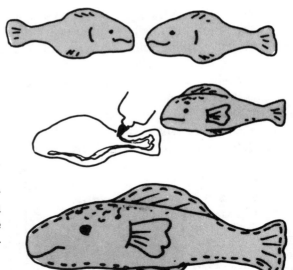

Use rubbing paper to apply pressure. Allow to dry overnight. (In some cases, add strength to the glue by stapling the sides together.)

9. The following day, have students take newspaper, crumple it up sheet by sheet, and push it into the open mouth of the fish or whale. Use the end of a broom handle or a ruler to push the paper down into the gullet. Do not use too much pressure or the seams will burst. Continue this until the paper protrudes toward the mouth cavity. Glue and staple the mouth area, leaving only a small opening. Allow to dry for awhile, and then complete the operation by stuffing the paper into the outer mouth area. Close this seam with a stapler.

10. To hang the fish or whale in balance, find two equally distant areas on bodies of large fish; for very large forms, three might be needed. Use a paper punch and punch a hole through both pieces of the paper bodies. For added strength, place some tape between the paper sides of the fish and make sure the punched hole goes through the tape. Carefully tie string through the holes.

11.

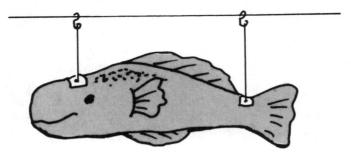

With custodial or other adult help, hang the fish or whales from light fixtures in the room. Use an opened paper clip tied to a string. After all the fish or whales have been hung, the students can add to the display by making seaweed for added color and realism.

140

Using a square scrap of paper, students can cut out a rough circle, then begin a spiral cut until the center is reached. Pull out the spiral. Cut out some leaf-like shapes and paste to the edges of the spiral. These can be added to the lights between the fish and whales.

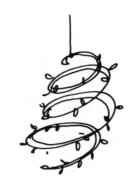

FOLLOW-UP

Art

As mentioned earlier, this is a fine adjunct to a room mural on undersea life.

Science

The research and studying that led up to the large fish constructions can be put into a report that can be read to the class and displayed along with the project.

Language Arts

Stories can be written about imaginary encounters with fish and whales. Refer to Captain Ahab's encounter with Moby Dick; Hemingway's *Old Man and the Sea;* and, of course, *Jaws.*

Observing Sea Life

Leading U.S. aquariums include:

Monterey Bay Aquarium
886 Cannery Row
Monterey, CA 93940

New England Aquarium
Central Wharf off Atlantic Avenue
Boston, MA 02110

New York Aquarium
W. Eighth and Surf Avenue
Coney Island, Brooklyn, NY 11224

John B. Shedd Aquarium
1200 Lake Shore Drive
Chicago, IL 60605

National Aquarium
Pier 3, 501 E. Pratt Street
Baltimore, MD 21202

Books

The following books are wonderful resources: *Rescue of the Stranded Whales* by Kenneth Mallory and Andrea Conley (Simon & Schuster); *Sharks and Whales* by Burton Albert, for ages 7-10 (The Putnam and Grosset Group); and *Whales, the Gentle Giants* by Joyce Milton, for ages 6-9 (Random House).

This mural project is at its best when several disciplines are employed simultaneously. The base is a major art project of considerable scale and content. But the content cannot be superficial. It must be carefully researched and presented. It should have a wealth of supportive visual and hard factual information available for research. The generalized outline presented in the next few pages applies to any number of themes. All art materials and methods of presentation are the same. What changes is the subject matter. What follows, then, is a list description of some of the most successful themes for this undertaking:

1. *Journey to a Distant Planet;* or *Man's First Step on Mars;* or *A Strange Journey to NI* (Neptune's third moon discovered in 1989); or *Does the 10th Planet—Planet X—Exist?;* or *Beyond the Milky Way, Journey to the Andromeda Galaxy. . .* the titles are endless, but topics about space travel are always received enthusiastically.

The mural is best approached from a basis of fact, a strictly scientific survey of the vast amount of information obtained by the NASA and Soviet space probes, especially the work of the Discoverer vehicles, all beautifully presented in the *National Geographic.* For example, it can present the possible landing on a surface of a known planet or satellite, using all of the technology now known and used by the United States' moon landing. Such a mural could depict the region around one planet or aspects of this entire solar system. The possibilities here are also endless in terms of fine-tuning a specific theme. On the other end of the spectrum, the mural would move into a purely imaginary and fantasy world where the planets, space vehicles, and assorted nonhumans could fully explore the world of science fiction. The choice is yours. For best science, math, and language arts correlations, we suggest the first approach, although both have value.

2. Titles of another theme could be *Life Under the Sea;* or *Undersea Life in the Indian Ocean;* or *Beneath the Gulf by the Mississippi;* or *Off the Atlantic;* or *Game Fish Species in California;* or *Mammals of the Sea;* or *The Endangered Whales of the North Atlantic;* etc. This theme has as much content to explore as the previous major theme. It is best done with a strong preparatory base that relies upon interdisciplinary programming that includes art, science, history, and social studies. The stress could be on food species exclusively, their life cycle, means of migration, how they are caught, etc. Another direction could be the conserving of whale populations found along both coasts.

3. *America's National Forests;* or *National Parks and Seashores;* or *The Deserts of the Southwest;* or *The Great Plains States;* or *The Everglades of Florida;* etc., are titles of a theme that would stress a particular region and explore the geographic as well as natural characteristics. This would include wildlife, natural phenomenon, vegetation, etc. It could also include contemporary concerns, the cities of the regions, manufacturing, ethnic areas, etc. The theme can be scaled to include only the local region of the class, or the mural can consist of several parts and cover a variety of regions. If possible, a visit to a local natural history museum would be helpful.

4. Another theme is *Life in Our Town—Yesterday, Today and Tomorrow* (town meaning city, neighborhood, region, island, etc.). Here is the perfect local history project that can include recent events or those of another time. Cover the major features of the community, its people, homes, food supplies, businesses, parks, schools, major buildings, etc. This can all be supported by an array of written material of anecdotes, histories, current events, etc.

Additional themes might be:
  5. *The Four Seasons* (individually or as four panels)
  6. *North American Wildlife*
  7. *The Jungles of South America*
  8. *African Village Life*
  9. *Life in Ancient Egypt*
  10. *Springtime in the Netherlands*
  11. *Life in Ancient Pompeii*
  12. *Eskimo Life in Arctic Regions*
  13. *Old and New China or Japan*

The list can be extended indefinitely. What is important to realize is that the procedures for making any of the above murals will be more or less the same and will employ the same materials and sequences. What will vary will be the content. The dinosaur mural directions given here include the sequences and the structure to be used in the development of any theme.

DINOSAURS—GIANT REPTILES FROM THE PAST (1-6)

A dinosaur mural creates an exciting large room or hallway environmental display that makes a blockbuster impression when first viewed. Besides being visually impressive, it provides students with an opportunity to work on a very large scale and teaches them the proportionate relationships between objects and space. This display beautifully combines art, science, mathematics, and language arts.

OBJECTIVES

Art
  • Correctly render object shapes using research materials.
  • Use various coloring agents in sequence to recreate the color, texture, and feel of the natural objects in the picture plane of the mural.
  • Increase drawing skills so that corrections and additions are few and easily done.
  • Use arrangement and compositional skills to make the environments as real and lifelike as possible.

Math
  • Learn about the proportion and scale of objects through research.
  • Discover size relationships among objects and surroundings.
  • Compute the weight of dinosaurs or height of mountains, etc.

Science
  • Read scientific research to learn about life forms in a particular environment.
  • Have the theme of the mural include the study of weather, climate, and season.

Language Arts
  • Relate science, math, and art skills to descriptive writing and reporting.
  • Develop fictional stories about aspects of the life depicted in the murals.
  • Write and perform a short play using the mural for a theme and set.
  • Create poems about the mural.
  • Use the murals as "discoveries" upon which to develop journalistic reporting.

Social Studies
- Learn about lifestyle in a particular time and place

MATERIALS NEEDED

- Covering for desks
- 9″ × 12″ newsprint
- Pencils and erasers
- Markers
- Wax crayons
- Tempera paints in all primary and secondary colors plus white and black
- Water cans
- Plastic containers for pallettes
- Coffee cans for paint mixing
- 3″ and 4″ sponge applicators
- 12″ × 18″ 80-lb construction paper in various colors
- 60-lb tan kraft paper in 36″ and 48″ rolls
- Scissors
- Rulers
- Yardsticks
- Staplers and staples
- White glue and newsprint rubbing paper
- Scrap newspaper
- #2, #6, #10 brushes in 2″ and 3″ widths
- White chalk and erasers
- Ladders

PREPARATION

For any of these mural projects, preliminary preparation is absolutely necessary. You or a group of teachers should have accumulated a wealth of supportive materials that include books on the subject, prints, films, film strips, slides, television tapes, etc. You should also have previously measured the space where the mural will be hung/assembled. It is very important to know both the total height and width of the space as well as how the mural will be attached to the wall surface. For example, Can it be stapled? Can masking tape be used? Will a custodian prepare a nailing lattice to support the work, if the walls cannot receive either staples or tape? All of these things must be considered before beginning. These murals are wonderful team projects and can incorporate group skills. Besides reviewing the space, have a clear idea of what concepts and what outcomes are desired. The success of the project depends on the attitude and participation of all the *teachers*. Rather than look upon this as just a mural project, teachers should envision the undertaking as a major interdisciplinary and correlated project. At the completion, it is an impressive presentation for parents and for students from other classes. It also could be a community event.

DIRECTIONS

1. Dinosaurs, those marvelous creatures that roamed our planet fill everyone with awe. Begin the motivation for this lesson (if any is necessary) by using film strips, a film, slides, prints—any information about prehistoric creatures to stimulate thinking. Good preparation is essential. Prepare students to

imagine the earth, from 200,000,000 to 65,000,000 years ago. Discuss the earth's environment at this period of time. Elicit information from the students about the climate, weather, abundant rain forests, and vegetation. Then delve into the vast periods of time in which the dinosaurs lived and how different species evolved. Introduce the concept of paleontology, climactic studies, fossil research on a worldwide basis, and the discoveries still being made. Introduce some mathematical guidelines. Discuss the size and weight of these creatures. Make comparisons with current life forms. Make comparisons with objects and masses in and around school space. Supply as much information as possible in the initial phase to generate interest.

2. To enhance the mood, develop a time warp story about some students who find themselves in the time and place of the activity.

3. Ask the students how they would design an immense mural for the room or hallway that would picture this fascinating time. Discuss briefly what murals are and how they have been used for interior and exterior decorations and messages for many years. Refer to the decorated rooms of Paestum and Pompeii from Roman times; the walls of many Egyptian tombs; the Bayeux tapestry; the Vatican; the political murals of the Mexicans, Orozco and Rivera; and, of course, the murals of the American depression that appear in many public buildings from the 1930's. Perhaps there is one in your town. Discuss the background space and its breakdown into fore-, middle-, and background. Ask what might be found in each area, based on their research. The background would include a steamy tropical sky, maybe distant mountains, and perhaps even a volcano. The middleground would include the swamp or fern marsh with distant vistas of tropical plant growth, water plants, etc. The foreground would include tall fern-like trees, hanging vines, etc. Ask some students to go to the chalkboard and roughly draw a Cretaceous forest. Have the students discuss the results. Encourage input that includes both the scientific and artistic aspect of the sketches.

4. With 48″ paper (or any other desired size), take three separate sheets the length of the full mural and roll them out onto the floor. Have three or four students each select the ground they would like to do. Use white chalk to outline the basic natural shapes. Make corrections. Use reference texts on paleontology and botany 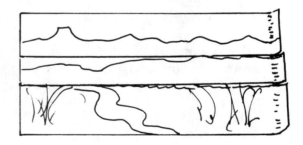 so that students can learn to approximate and record the actual shapes of objects. NOTE: In this instance and with other themes, it is necessary to use considerable published information as references. Try to discourage students from copying exactly what they see. Instead, encourage them to use the information for resource, but let their own drawing skills prevail. The difference between copied work and original skills is a difficult gray area, but it can be learned with continual teacher overseeing.

5. With the preliminary drawings done, demonstrate how to mix and apply paint. With large areas of paper to cover, show students how to mix large amounts of paint in coffee cans and then water them down so that the consistency is not too heavy. After the paint has been mixed, demonstrate how to apply it. The first applications of paint will be for broad flat surfaces and not for details. Use the 2″ or 3″ brushes, or better, the 4″ sponge brushes. For the sky, use blues to light blues to pinks and yellow-pinks near the horizon. Paint darkest blues at top and blend the changes as you work towards the horizon. At the horizon, paint the mountains in mauves or light violets, changing into violet and greens. For the middleground, an irregular edge will suggest mid-level vegetation, the swamp water, and floating plants. Just the broadest of outlined shapes will be painted at first. For the foreground, paint the marsh swamp edge, the bases of ferns, reeds, etc. The top will also have an irregular edge and will be placed over the middleground. After the large sheets have received their first coats of paint; let them dry overnight. (They can be neatly rolled up when completed and dry, and then unrolled.)

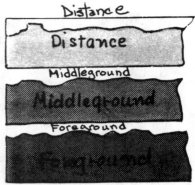

6. Mix as much of the paint as possible before beginning. Place newspaper underneath the entire kraft paper area before starting. Have a floor painting station. Take several sheets of wide newspaper and place the paint, brushes, sponges, paper towels, and a damp rag to wipe up drops and spills on the newspaper. NOTE: It is fun and sometimes helps if students work in stocking feet. This prevents wear and tear on the surface of the kraft paper and lessens chances for spills.

7. When the three stations are set, challenge the students to check on their drawings and begin work with the paint. Check their progress and give assistance where needed. Especially check on the consistency and amount of water in the paint. Keep these within reasonable limits so that the paper surface is not damaged.

8. When complete, let it dry, and then roll it up for next time. Put materials away. For the next session, set up newspaper and a work station. Use palettes for mixing colors for details such as plants on the water, flying insects, flowers in the swamp, clouds, etc. Markers and crayons can also be used, but only when the paint is dry.

9. While this is being done, other groups can be working on objects (e.g., tall ferns, trees, vines, etc.) that will be placed in semi-relief on top of the kraft background. Draw the objects on 24″ or 36″ long lengths of the kraft paper and then paint them in. They will run horizontally over the three levels in the background.

10. When dry at the end of the day, tack up to wall or roll them *very* loosely. At the next session, roll out and add details. NOTE: Follow the same prepara-

146

tion procedures. Use newspaper and a painting work station, but mix smaller amounts of paint.

11. Now for the dinosaurs. Present the information on the dinosaurs from a firm historical viewpoint. Try to keep the various ages chronologically correct, and try not to mix up species that lived in different periods. Employ either ground work or have the students make lists of the many types that existed at one time and/or place. Use research uncovered from the American work in the western U.S. After the list has been made, introduce a math lesson on proportion. Take the largest form and work up a scale. Use a ratio of 1″ per foot or ½″ per foot to determine the scale of the creatures. For example, if a brontosaurus is found to be 100′ in length, you might use a sheet of paper 100″ long with a corresponding height of 50″ or so. White glue can be used to attach two sheets together where necessary. Using the available information, determine the sizes of 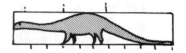 the creatures. Make a list of their names on a chalkboard and place sizes next to each. The students can select the creature they would like make, or groups of two can work together. More than one of each creature can be made. Also, a mural 30′ feet or more in length introduces the concept of distance and size relationships. Those objects farther away will be smaller than those close by. Discuss the skin texture of these creatures, and use current information relating to lizards that exist today. After the discussions have the students measure the paper needed.

12. After the groups have been established or students have been paired, begin work with the chalk drawing. Make corrections. Prepare general paint colors at paint stations. (NOTE: Move desks aside so that students can work on the floor. This always works well.) Prepare newspaper around kraft paper and begin painting. Do just the base color. Allow it to dry and begin detail work later. Use sponges, markers, and crayons to bring out individual features of each animal. All the while, you should be circulating about the room and giving assistance where needed. Call attention to the fidelity of the shape, based on the research. After each child or partnership has selected their creature, they should begin research. Use a small individual card listing the size, eating habits, etc., as a reference. Before work is done, tack up the dinosaurs. Hold a class critique. Ask which ones need more work and what can be done to improve them. Try to raise the level of work to the highest point.

13. When the dinosaurs are complete, think of other objects that can be introduced. Draw small creatures, flowers, vines, etc., on the colored construction paper with the markers, crayons, and paint, and cut them out with scissors.

14. Now that all parts of the mural have been completed, it is time to begin assembly. There are two ways to do this. The irregular strips of both the middle- and foregrounds have to be cut out. (Follow cutting practices mentioned previously.) The strips can either be glued in sequence with the white glue or the backs can be taped together with masking tape. Staple the mural to the wall if possible. If the entire mural is to hang, it must be glued together. Apply small amounts along the edges, overlap, apply pressure with the rubbing paper and allow it to dry for at least several hours. (In a crowded classroom, it is best to let it dry overnight and hang it the following morning.)

15. If the mural is to hang from a rod or lattice, the pieces must be glued down before hanging. Otherwise, they can be stapled on after the mural has been attached to the wall. The arranging is a major learning lesson. Clear the desks and chairs from the floor. Remove shoes. Gather all the completed objects and begin to arrange them in the sequence desired. The largest creatures  will be in the foreground. Large creatures that are far away will appear small and will be placed higher on the picture plane. Several of the same species might be grazing together. Pteranodons might be flying in the sky. Several flesh eaters might be devouring a carcass of a downed prey. Smaller reptiles might be running through the foreground. larger ferns might overlap others. Vines would hang from the top, etc. The possibilities are endless. Before gluing, arrange all pieces and make it a lesson about composition. Check several times, until the arrangement seems correct. Involve the entire class in the activity. When agreement has been reached on the composition, mark placement with chalk and begin the gluing. Fold back those farthest away and apply glue. Use rubbing paper to adhere. NOTE: It is not necessary to remove all items and glue from the back up. If care is taken, many can be glued where they rest. Smaller ones can be lifted off, glued at a glue station and put back in place. It is important to remember the overlapping.

16. Complete the gluing, again at the end of a day. Then it can be hung after first checking for details that need to be added. These may include blood from an encounter, details obliterated by the gluing, items that were forgotten, etc. Now hang the mural. Gently unroll. If the mural is 30′ × 12′, ladders will be needed. Use staples for the lattice or strong tape.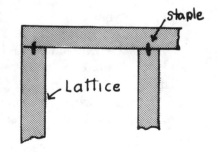

Tack the top edge down, working from one end to the other. Gently let the mural unroll and tack the other sides down. It is complete!

FOLLOW-UP

Art

Prepare a display of book illustrations from many of the noted (published) artists who have worked on dinosaur drawings and paintings.

Math

• Prepare a math display of relative sizes. Do some line drawings of popular dinosaurs, and then provide contemporary counterparts for a comparison of sizes. Do the same for bulk mass and weight.

• Use a model of the school building or the building itself to show the scale of a Brontosaurus. Figure out the height and length of the building, and use windows, and doors to show which parts of the dinosaur would fall on which parts of the school building.

Science

• Extend the small research cards into full-length reports about the individual dinosaurs. Record all pertinent material.

• Prepare an exhibit on paleontology. Gather some old bones, rocks, etc., and illustrate how scientists can determine the age of objects in fossil beds and extrapolate the ages of dinosaurs.

• Gather current research on the demise of the great lizards 65,000,000 years ago. Prepare a report or a diagram.

• Report on recent findings, such as the Epanterias near Masonville, Colorado. The Epanterias were as large as the Tyrannosaurus rex. Write to Dr. Robert T. Bakker at the University of Colorado in Boulder for more information.

• Visit Dinosaur Quarry near Holyoke, Massachusetts to see dinosaur footprints; Dinosaur State Park near Hartford, Connecticut; Dinosaur National Monument in Colorado; Dinosaur Valley State Park in Texas. You can also visit "Dinosaur Day" events on Central Park's Great Lawn in New York City, in early June.

Language Arts

• Write a report from those listed in this activity and an extension could work into more creative areas. Write stories using the previously mentioned time warp theme. These stories could be made into fuller stories with cliff-hangers (like old time movie serials).

• Write poems about "humanized" dinosaurs.

• Ask for "what if" stories; for example, "What if we discovered a living dinosaur living in Lake Champlain?"

Books

The following are wonderful resources: *The News About Dinosaurs* by Patricia Lauber (Bradbury Press); *All About Dinosaurs* by Q. L. Pearce, includes a poster (Simon & Schuster); and *The Big Golden Book of Dinosaurs* (Western Publishing).

Activity 45 ============================ NATIVE AMERICANS— A DIORAMA (2-6)

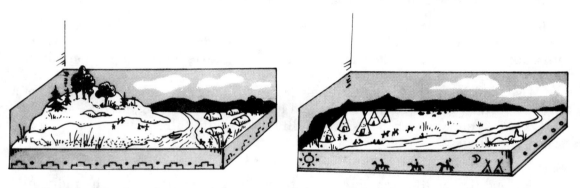

Combine the fun of creating a large-scale diorama with the study of the variety and wealth of Indian village activities in the U.S. during the colonial and federal periods. This project can provide the visual impact of Native Americans' cultural contributions. Students will have a number of manipulative and interpretive challenges.

OBJECTIVES

Art

♦ Make a scale model called a diorama.

♦ Learn about three-dimensional forms in nature and how to replicate these forms using a variety of materials.

♦ Organize a given space that will mimic a real one, working on a reduced scale.

♦ Employ and assemble a wide variety of natural and man-made materials that depend on good cutting and construction skills.

History, Geography, and Social Studies

♦ Learn about the geographical regions of the United States as they exist today and as they existed when peopled by early Indian cultures.

♦ Refine map-making skills and map-reading skills.

150

- Learn about the differences in various cultures, their government, rituals, living conditions, associations, lore, language, decorative arts, etc.
- Refine study skills by undertaking research on selected tribes.

Language Arts
- Improve reporting skills by developing reports on Native American life.
- Write prose or poetry based on Indian folklore or way of life.
- Read aloud parts of the poem HIAWATHA by Henry Wadsworth Longfellow.

Archaeology
- Learn about basic archaeological principles and methods.

MATERIALS NEEDED

The following materials will be needed by the class. This is essentially a group project. Its several parts can be split among various groups. Use the listed materials as a resource center.

- 4′ × 8′ (or other size) homosote or plywood
- Tables or saw horses on which to set plywood
- 12′ or 15′ long (or less depending on plywood size) of kraft paper
- Poster or tempera paints in browns, tans, blues, whites, greens
- 2″, 3″, 4″ brushes and sponges
- Cans for water
- Dry grass clippings
- Colored markers or pencils
- Thread, twine, needles
- Plasticene or plasti-clay in natural, terra cotta, stone, and various other colors
- Red ceramic clay
- Toothpicks
- Craft sticks
- Green sapling branches
- Rocks, sand, dry earth
- Kraft paper scraps or brown wrapping paper
- Sheeting scraps
- White glue
- Green construction paper
- Dry branch pieces
- Newspapers
- Scraps of fur
- Scissors

PREPARATION

This is a very complex lesson. The first decision is which Indian culture and region to use as the basis for the project. We suggest you use that region most closely associated with the students in the class. Florida students, for example, might wish to cover the Indians of the Southeast, particularly the Seminoles. Students living in east coastal Massachusetts might wish to cover the woodland tribes of the Northeast, especially the Wampanoags. Those living in the Northern Plains might cover the Sioux, and so on.

Once the decision has been made, everything else will fall into place. Considerable preparation should be done by you. Film strips, films, slides, publications, articles, tapes, etc., should be assembled from both school and local community resources. It would also be very appropriate to have photo examples of dioramas, particularly those from the New York Museum of Natural History, which provide excellent examples of what the thrust of the project might be. NOTE: The activity described here uses the Indian cultures of the Eastern Woodlands. This will differ from those of other regions, but research will and should uncover pertinent information and differences.

DIRECTIONS

1. Challenge the students to list some of the many contributions our country today can trace to early Native Americans. Play a matching game by compiling two lists of related objects and have the students match items from each. Hold up objects that are related; for example, a paddle (for a canoe); pancakes (for maple syrup projects); and then move into popcorn and corn products, tobacco, tomatoes, potatoes, lacrosse, basket making, etc. Research should make the list as comprehensive as possible.

2. Tell the students that it would be nice to honor these ancestors by creating a living scene of what life was like in a typical village in the region selected, at a particular period of time. Go to the chalkboard, and make a list of headings for major components: shelter and homes, people, clothing, food gathering and preparation, geography (typography), village life, transportation, weaving, etc. Have students sign up under various headings. These groups can then choose a leader and begin the task of researching the general characteristics of the tribe as well as those specific ones relating to the headings. NOTE: We suggest that the correlated aspects of this project (the work on history, geography, language arts, etc.) be undertaken before the physical studio work. This can take the form of written reports, illustrated cards to accent the final project, charts with illustrations to hang around the diorama, or anything else in a similar vein. When these are completed, work can begin on the first phase of the diorama.

3. DIORAMA—FIRST PHASE: Have all materials ready. Rest the homosote on some available tables or desks. Butt it up close to a wall. Have the students responsible for the work on geography/topography take white chalk and roughly lay out the village and region. Consider the best site for the village—by a river or other water source, near woods, in the highlands, etc. High areas can be made with kraft paper with newspaper stuffing. It is easier to first paint the kraft paper with a base color and add other colors for variations. After the paper is dry, crumple it and staple it to the area drawn on the board. Leave a section open to insert the newspaper. After this is done, staple shut. Discuss the result with the students. Take suggestions and then make changes. With this complete, place newspaper beneath the board and begin mixing paints for the board's surface. Use large brushes and sponges to fill in appropriate colors for water areas, uplands, grass areas, and forests. Allow the paint to dry before adding details. While this is being done, roll out a length of kraft paper 18″ or

24″ in width, and place over the newspaper on the floor. Mix sky and cloud colors. Use large brushes to apply the first color. Allow to dry and then add clouds. (If storms or rain conditions are desired, use the appropriate gray colors.) Add distant mountains and hills that blend with foreground. Put sky paper away to dry.

4. When the basic colors on the board are dry, mix other colors with white glue in a container and add soil. Place this mixture on top of some ground areas for texture. For other areas, apply white glue directly, and sift or shake dry soil on top. Try the same with gravel, stones, sand, dry grass, etc., whatever is desired to create a natural surface that mimics land surface-changes. Glue the rocks in place. Let the entire surface dry. When done, attach the sky to the wall surface around one half of the exhibit. Then place the board back into place.

5. SECOND PHASE—SHELTER HOUSING: Shelter housing depends upon the region. For the Plains states and in some areas of the East, tepees were used. The materials varied. Several dry sticks, tree branches, or grapevine pieces can be tied together with natural twine. The coverings can mimic either hides or bark. Actual slivers of tree bark can be sewn or glued together. If not available, use torn pieces of kraft paper sheets and stain them with a tinted water, crumple them, unfold, and let dry. These pieces can mimic hides. After drying, decorations can be added with markers. These can be sewn together or pasted with marker "stitches" and then attached to the sticks. One side can be lifted for an entry way.

In much of the East, the most usual form of shelter was the long house or wigwam. Take four saplings or grapevine pieces, cut, and bend them to the same size. Form half circles. Plan the size of the wigwam base. Take four stiff limbs, cut to size, and lash them together with twine.

Lash the bent saplings to the base. Take two more saplings and lash them to the wigwam frame. See the following illustration for placement. Work with diorama size in mind.

Covering can be made the same as mentioned above. Bark pieces can be used or kraft paper can be stained to look like hide. Further authenticity can be obtained by choosing a summer covering and using small lengths of reeds or grasses. These can be pasted to kraft paper, cut into lengths, and attached by sewing or gluing to the frame. A hole should be cut into the top as was the custom for wigwams or long houses for removing the smoke of indoor fires.

6. THIRD PHASE—FIGURES: To maintain the look of authenticity of the diorama, the figures will be in scale with the wigwams/tepees and land layout. They should be no more than several inches high, fitting into a tepee or wigwam doorway. Demonstrate how to make figures with the plasticene. Review basic figure constructions. Have a student stand and move about; talk about joints and major body segments (head, upper body, hips, lower and upper arms, thighs, lower legs, hands, feet, etc.). Refer to Activity 28, The Go For It Sports Figures. Using pliable plasticene, form a figure. Check the proportions and establish an attitude for the figure. Keep the figure in place by using toothpicks and a base of plasticene. This is the rough figure. When it is complete, add details. Use other colored pieces of plasticene for facial features and hair. Add bits and pieces of fabric for clothing. These can be pressed into the clay or attached using a fine twine or thread. Several figures can be completed without the toothpicks. These might be seated figures or figures on horses made of the same plastic material. Use toothpicks or pieces of toothpicks to set the pose in place. Refer to illustrations in research material for clothing styles and decorations. Strive for authenticity and proportion.

7. FOURTH PHASE—ANIMAL LIFE: By using the plasticene, students can tackle the problem of modeling animals indigenous to a particular region.

For example, the Woodland Indians of the East encountered buffalo (yes, buffalo in the East), deer, bears, wolves, eagles, salmon, shad, herring, etc. The unit of measurement for the animal size should be the human figure. As modeling progresses, insert toothpicks for stability. Scraps of fur can be added for even greater authenticity. Put aside.

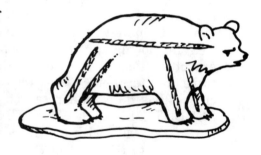

8. FIFTH PHASE—DETAILS: These are the elements that will bring the diorama to life.

   a. *Trees, bushes, etc.:* Actual examples can be gathered from real plant life. Winter branches can be given a spring look by finely cutting green pieces of paper and applying to branches covered with white glue. Stabilize the branches with a base of plasticene. Use the same procedure for bushes. Segments of branches can be used for campfires along with stones and pebbles.

   b. *Pottery:* The same plasticene can be used to form pottery. If possible, use ceramic clay, which can be fired. Once again, research will determine the forms and decoration needed, and the size of the figures will determine the size of the pottery.

   c. *Special areas:* These include weaving areas, hide tanning and stretching, baking ovens, gardens, tobacco drying, ritual areas, etc. Students can be challenged to try their hands at these most unusual constructions using the same selection of varied materials from the list. Refer to Activity 47 for weaving information.

9. SIXTH PHASE—ASSEMBLY: At this point, you have made all of the major components—shelters, figures, animals, trees, bushes, pottery, etc. The students are now challenged to use their research to put all of the individual items into a logical arrangement that will accurately depict the culture, the regions, and the life style of the tribe(s) in a particular time. With your guidance, a wide-ranging discussion can be held. The thrust of the talk should be about the concept to be shown. Such things as the placement of the village, its access to water, placement of outbuildings, gardens in relation to fishing areas, forests, grasslands, etc., have to be determined. All students can participate in the initial phases of placing objects on the board. Discussions can continue about what the class wishes the figures to be doing. One concept would be to capture a single, ordinary day in the life of a simple village. The figures could be hunting, fishing, preparing fires, using and making canoes,

155

tanning hides, tending tobacco or corn crops, or preparing for a ceremony. Children could be running about or fishing. The list is endless. All students can participate in this. The final details can be added: pottery, animals, the weaving loom, hunting weapons, etc. *Stop* all work as it nears conclusion, and check for any missed details. Perhaps some soil is needed, or more grass, trees, shelters, etc. Fine tune the whole setting, and let the students make choices based on their research.

10. SEVENTH PHASE—THE FINISHING TOUCH: Roll out a length of kraft paper. Decorate with paint, using Indian symbols or pictographs, and attach the paper to the edge of the board as a skirt to give the diorama a finished look. (See the two illustrations at the beginning of this activity.)

FOLLOW-UP

History and Language Arts

•   Employ the same level of research and examination of materials to develop a project of contemporary Indian life in the region you live in or in some other selected region. Uncover information about reservations, the Department of Indian Affairs of the U.S. Government, current Indian life styles, schooling, traditions, and business practices. Consider those tribes that have benefitted from the use of their reservations for the development of oil, the generation of electrical power, the salmon fishing industry, gaming, and arts and crafts. Consider current Indian problems and the efforts underway to address them. Prepare written reports based on the research. Report how the Quinault Indians of Wash. State have organized their self-rule experiment.

•   Research the efforts being made by many national tribes to keep their culture and history intact. Study the writings of contemporary Indians, their poetry, their art, etc. Develop a presentation. Invite some local person who has a knowledge of Indian culture, which he or she would consider sharing with the students.

•   A full-scale Indian resource center is being built in New Jersey. Located in Westhampton Township in Burlington County, it is in the Philadelphia-Camden area. The village will be a reproduction of a traditional Powatan village of around year 1500. At the museum will be dioramas of Indian life throughout the U.S., rotating exhibits from all the country's tribes, and the continuation of the yearly Arts Festival held there every October at the Rancocas Indian Reservation. Full-size wigwams have been built on the site. The Indians working on this center are also eager to tell how they live in today's world. For information on donating time or money to the museum, call Chief Roy Crazy Horse at (609) 261-4747.

Art

•   Undertake another diorama using the same materials listed in the activity and depict some aspect of current Indian life. For example, show the salmon fishing industry in the Northwest, the jewelry and crafts of the Southwest tribes, pine nut gathering of the Pyote, the oil development in Oklahoma, the building expertise of the Iroquois of New York City, etc.

•   Prepare a formal presentation of the Native American diorama and invite the community.

•   Undertake a weaving project as described in Activities 46 through 48 using Indian motifs.

- Classes in the metropolitan New York City area can plan to visit the Museum of the American Indian, Broadway and 155th Street (212) 283-2420 and the American Museum of Natural History, Central Park West at 79th Street (212) 769-5000.

Books

You might want to check into the *Indians of North America* series published by Chelsea House Publishers, 95 Madison Avenue, New York, New York 10016.

Magazines

Take a look at the March 1989 issue of *National Geographic* for the article "Indian Burial Grounds: Who Owns Our Past?"

Activity 46 ══════════ UNDER AND OVER COLORED LINES—INTRODUCING WEAVING (3-6)

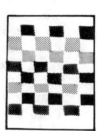

This colorful paper construction project introduces the children to the basics of weaving and pattern forming. Its visual impact will challenge them to try fiber weaving.

OBJECTIVES

Art
- Understand the mechanics of weaving.
- Understand that line is the primary design element in weaving.
- Use cutting and pasting skills.
- Improve manipulative skills.

Math
- Measure accurately.
- Learn how to plot in sequence.

MATERIALS NEEDED

- Covering for desks
- Rulers
- Scissors
- Pencils and Erasers
- White glue and applicators
- Rubbing paper

- 80-lb rectangular construction paper in various colors cut to 12″ × 18″ for the loom/warp
- Strips of ½ ″ and ¼ ″ wide construction paper (for weft) in various colors

PREPARATION

Make a demonstration model in advance to show the students. Cut a large number of ½ ″ and ¼ ″ strips of colored paper. The ¼ ″ strips should contrast when used in over and counter weaving. When constructing the model, use harmonious colors. Also use one color in a repeat design to add interest.

DIRECTIONS

1. Introduce the lesson by explaining that weaving is the interlacing of fibers or paper. The *loom* is the support structure on which they are woven. The vertical paper strips are called the *warp* and the strip that will be woven under and over the warp is called the *weft*. Show the model as you explain.

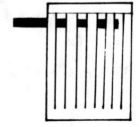

2. Take the model and point out that the design is created by the horizontal colors of the weft as they lock into the color of the warp. Show that the use of repeated colors can add interest to the design, and demonstrate the concept of pattern. (Refer to the illustration at the beginning of this activity.)
3. Hand out the materials and ask the students to cover their desks. Tell them that they will be following you as you work, and they need to follow directions carefully in a step-by-step manner.
4. Take the 12″ × 18″ paper and hold it up vertically. This will become your loom. The shorter sides will be the top and bottom.
5. Take the bottom edge and match to the top edge, with the corners matching exactly. Fold along the bottom.
6. Take the ruler and measure a line 1″ below the top edge. Make this a bold line parallel to the edge.

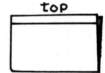

7. Turn the paper sideways and rule equally spaced ½ ″ lines from the fold to the bold 1″ line.

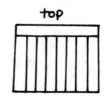

8. Stop the class and review all work. Students who made mistakes by folding or ruling incorrectly can redo on the reverse side.
9. Hold the folded paper firmly with fold at bottom; take the scissors and cut along the ruled lines from the fold edge to the bold line. *Do not cut beyond.* Open the paper and place flat upon the desk. This is the loom with the warp strips.

10. Let the children select the ½ " strip colors they wish to use.
11. Select a ½ " strip to be your weft. Begin weaving under, over, under, over, etc. Tell the children to follow.

12. Select a second strip and reverse the order—over, under, over, under, etc. Carefully push each added strip as close as possible to one preceding it. Keep evaluating the color choices.
13. Repeat the procedure until the loom is filled. The weft strips have completed a woven surface called the *woof.* (This word will no doubt bring a period of laughter in the class!) Have the students carefully align all the weft strips.
14. Now that the base weaving is completed, the students can continue learning over weaving. Over weaving is the placing of the ¼" strips over the weft strips. Copy this figure onto the chalkboard for all to see. Have the children select their ¼" strips. Begin the weaving, telling the children that patience and dexterity are needed.

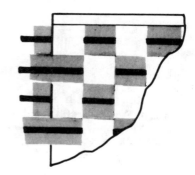

15. After the over weaving is completed, introduce counter weaving which is the weaving of the narrow strips over the woven area. Copy the following illustration onto the chalkboard. Tell the children to take the ¼ " strips and follow the drawing. When the weaving is completed, the narrow strips should be carefully centered. Take the glue and apply it sparingly to all end pieces, and use the rubbing paper to insure a good adhesion.

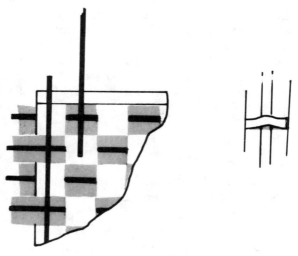

16. Take scissors and trim all strips to match the loom edges or let the ends extend for a fringe effect.

Art

Encourage students to continue paper weaving by constructing an irregular weaving project. Prepare the paper loom as before, except draw irregular, curved, freehand drawn warp lines from the bottom fold to the bold top line. *Do not draw the lines too close together.* Cut

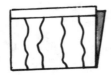

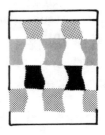

along the lines and open the loom, laying it flat on the desk. Take precut ½ " strips and weave as before. When completed, align the strips and glue in place.

After all the work is completed, the students can take a vote to see if they would like to make a big paper "patchwork" quilt out of their woven constructions. Arrange the weavings onto one large piece of background paper; dark blue or black would be best.

Activity **47** ══════════════════ **FUN WITH FIBER WEAVING (3-6)**

This project builds upon the paper weaving done in Activity 46, "Under and Over Colored Lines." Fiber weaving introduces the children to weaving with various textures and color combinations. The project can be used as a wall hanging or a purse. They will be studying the history and everyday uses of woven products. Helping to understand the subject and create enthusiasm are such books as *The Weaver's Gift* by Kathryn Lasky and *A History of Textiles* by Kay Wilson. You might also read such classics as the story of Rumpelstilskin and Penelope of the *Odyssey*.

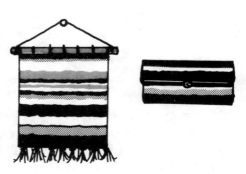

OBJECTIVES

Art
   • Understand that line is the element that creates the design.
   • Choose colors and textures that produce a pleasing combination of harmony and contrast.
   • Understand balance and repetition.
   • Work with the concept of pattern.
   • Experience making decorative and useful products.

Math
   • Plot and think in sequence.
   • Develop accurate measuring skills.

Science
- Learn about the making of synthetic textiles.
- Learn about the origins of natural fibers.

Social Studies
- Discover the everyday uses of woven fabrics.
- Learn about slave labor on the Southern cotton plantations and child labor in the Northern cotton mills.

Geography
- Use wall maps to identify the fiber-producing regions of the world.

History
- Learn the history of woven textiles from ancient to contemporary times.

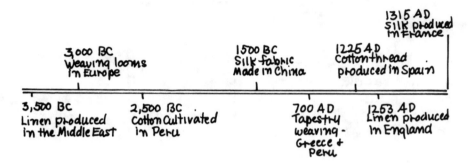

Language Arts
- Develop report-writing skills.

MATERIALS NEEDED

- Covering for desks
- Pencils
- Pattern-plan paper
- Rulers
- Sturdy scissors
- Masking tape
- ¼" dowel sticks
- A large assortment of fiber for weaving (string for warp, wool, cotton, flax, ribbon, synthetic yarn, and thick wool for fringe) NOTE: Make sure warp thread is of sufficient strength; test by pulling before using

- 10" × 16" or 12" × 18" sturdy cardboard (not corrugated) or chipboard for looms
- 12" × ½ " sturdy cardboard or chipboard for shuttle needles
- 3" × 1" sturdy cardboard or chipboard for bobbins
- Needles, pins, thread, buttons, beads, lining fabric, Velcro™, or snaps for the purse

PREPARATION

Obtain pictures of home spinning wheels and mill spinning machines that change raw material into fiber ready for the loom. Have a piece of burlap or any

161

other loosely woven fiber for demonstration. Inviting a local weaver to the classroom will add excitement to the project. Gather information on the history of the importance of woven cotton, wool and linen in the U.S. and the world. Some information sources are: Burlington Industries, Public Relations Service, 1345 Avenue of the Americas, New York, New York 10019; National Cotton Council of America, Memphis, Tennessee 38112; Wool Bureau, Inc., 360 Lexington Avenue, New York, New York 10017. Schools in the Washington, D.C. area can plan a field trip to the Textile Museum, 2320 S. Street N.W. Precut the cardboard pieces to save time and prevent accidents. Make and wind bobbins with lengths of fiber. Make shuttle needles and cut dowel sticks to measure slightly longer than the looms.

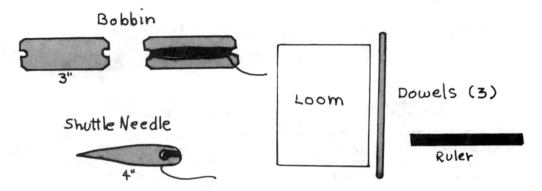

DIRECTIONS

1. Introduce weaving terms by writing them on the chalkboard:
   Weaving—the interlacing of fibers
   Loom—the support structure on which fibers are woven
   Warp—the fiber strung vertically on the loom
   Weft—the fiber used to produce the woof; the right-to-left or left-to-right binding of the warp threads
   Woof—the woven area created by the weft upon the warp
   Shuttle Needle—a carrier of short lengths of fiber
   Bobbin—the reel for holding and supplying the weft fibers
   Beater—the object to lift the warp fibers and also to press the woven lines together
   Sequence—the numerical plan of a pattern (for example: 1 under, 1 over, 3 under, 2 over) of the weft interlacing the warp strings
2. Show the students a loosely woven fabric such as burlap, and pull away some of the fibers to show its construction. Pass it around for all to see and feel. Show other fabric samples.
3. Using a wall map, ask students to identify the principal wool-, cotton-, flax-, silk-, and jute-producing areas of the world. Ask for a description of the climate and soil conditions as well as methods of production. Show audio-visuals of raw materials being converted into fiber ready for the loom.
4. Talk about the history of weaving from the ancient Egyptians and Native Americans, to the American introduction of denim. Plan a study of flax-cotton growing, wool and silk production, and fiber making through the years in

the U.S. (the role of textiles in the development of the country from 1620 to 1850, flax to silk). Divide the class into three groups, each researching a topic, such as "Life on a Southern Plantation," "Life in a New England Textile Mill Town," and "The Influence of Cotton on the Social and Political Life in the U.S."

5. Invite a local weaver to class to provide a demonstration.

6. Begin the activity by handing out the materials and asking the students to cover their desks. Each student receives all materials, except the wool, cotton, etc., and the purse materials. They will share the tape.

7. Ask the students to follow you carefully as you rule a *bold* pencil line across the top and bottom of the loom, measuring ½ " from the top and bottom edges.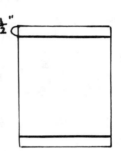

8. Measure and rule ½ " segments running perpendicular from the ruled bold lines to the loom's top and bottom edges. Take scissors and cut each of the segments *only to the bold lines*. These will form the notches for the warp string.

9. Take a long length of string and tie it around the first notch at the top. Extend the string directly to the first bottom notch. Loop the string around the back and pull to the front through the next notch.

10. Extend the string up to the next top notch and proceed until all the notches are filled. Tie the length at the last notch to the one preceding it.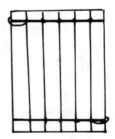

Check all work at this point. Keep the warp string tight. Instruct the children to take their dowel sticks and tape them to the sides of the loom. The dowels will help keep the tension even.

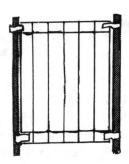

11. Now is the time to plan the weaving patterns. Students can take the paper and markers and work out a design to follow. Remind them that horizontal lines will produce the pattern. Have them repeat colors in various widths, giving balance and interest. Review Activity 5, "Elements of Design."

12. Now that the groundwork is done, allow the students to choose those colors and textures that will produce the look and feel they want.

13. Next ask them to lay the strung loom flat on the desk and take the ruler/beater or shuttle needle and place it *under* the first warp thread and *over* the second one and continue until the row is completed. Stand the ruler/beater on its side to separate the strings and move it to the center of the loom. This is called a shed and will enable the bobbin to move easily across the loom.

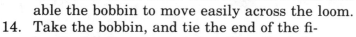

14. Take the bobbin, and tie the end of the fiber to the first warp string. Run the bobbin under the raised warp strings, completing the first line of weaving. Take the ruler/beater and weave it in the opposite direction. Weave *over* and then under, etc., and then stand it on end for the next line of the bobbin. Take the bobbin around the dowel for the return line. When attaching a new piece of yarn within the weaving area, work free-end into woven area and proceed to weave.

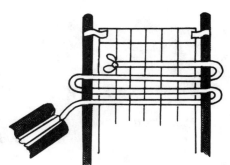

15. When a short length of fiber is to be used, use a threaded shuttle needle instead of a bobbin. When top and bottom designs are to match in width, turn the loom around and copy the top area. As weaving progresses, tell students to watch the tension so that it's not too tight nor too loose. Check to see that each line is close to the previous one and that everyone is using a beater (a ruler or a shuttle needle) to push each line in place. Loose fiber ends can be knotted together or skillfully tucked into the woven area. Continue to complete woof. Remove weaving by bending tabs and gently lift off warp threads.

16. When the weaving has been completed, ask who is making a wall hanging and who is making a purse. Those making a wall hanging will remove the work from the loom and take one of the dowel sticks and place it through the string loops. Attach a string to the dowel and hang it up for all to see and discuss. Ask the students if extra objects need to be sewn on for added interest. Perhaps fringe would complete the project. If fringe is to be added, cut 6″ lengths of thick wool for each fringe knot. These will be placed above the last line of the weaving. Each length will wrap around two warp threads and be pulled in place.

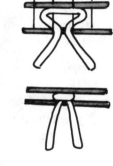

17. Each child who is making a purse will select a piece of lining fabric and lay it flat on the desk. The woven project will be placed on top of the lining that will be cut 1″ larger than the weaving.

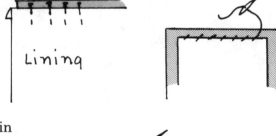

Tell the students to take the lining from underneath the the weaving, lay the lining on top of the weaving, and fold the lining edges inward, pin, and baste. After basting is done, sew the lining in place. Remove the basting.

Ask the students to fold the project in thirds, but the purse flap should be a little narrower. Sew the sides together. Then fasten a button and loop or Velcro™ or a snap for a fastening.

FOLLOW-UP

Art

• Suggest to the students that they make attractive woven placemats for gift-giving. These mats are made on 12″ × 15″ heavy cardboard looms. Each line is woven separately with no return. Keep lines close together when completed, and remove from the loom with much care. Have an adult machine-stitch along the length to give it stability. Cut the edges evenly.

Language Arts

Ask students of the three research groups in step 4 to write reports on their research. They can read these reports to the rest of the class.

Science

Encourage students interested in science to write a report and give a talk on the production of synthetic fibers. Some information sources are Celanese Fibers

Marketing Company, 522 Fifth Avenue, New York, New York 10036; and Du Pont de Nemours and Company, Wilmington, Delaware 19898.

History

Some students may want to write reports on the exalted place fabrics hold in most West African cultures south of the Sahara. Fabrics designate a person's social position, and fabric references abound in songs, proverbs and myths. Fabrics are also art forms and social symbols. For further details, write to the curator of The Dalton Gwatkin Textile Museum, 2320 S Street N.W., Washington, D.C. 20008 or call (202) 667-0441.

Resource

A good reference for your students to check is the May 1988 issue of *National Geographic* for the article, "Wool."

Activity 48 ═══════════════ WEAVING A PICTURE (3-6)

Weaving a picture? It can be done! It takes good planning and the results are simple but very effective designs that can be used as wall hangings. The more involved weaving technique challenges the students to progress in both designing and weaving skills.

OBJECTIVES

Art

- Review and reinforce basic weaving concepts.
- Learn more advanced weaving skills.
- Learn to plan a picture to weave.
- Understand the importance of fiber color tone in the color scheme.
- Understand the use of shape as the second most important design element.

MATERIALS NEEDED

- Covering for desks
- Design planning paper
- Black and colored markers
- Pencils
- Rulers
- String for warp
- Sturdy scissors
- Light- and dark-colored yarns and assorted fibers

- 10″ × 16″ or 12″ × 18″ sturdy cardboard (not corrugated) or chipboard for looms
- 12″ × ½ ″ sturdy cardboard or chipboard for shuttle needles
- 3″ × 1″ sturdy cardboard or chipboard for bobbins
- ¼″ dowel sticks
- String

PREPARATION

Make two models in advance that will illustrate the different stages in creating the project. One will have only the background completed and the other will be the completed project. Also show examples of picture plans. Precut the cardboard looms, shuttle needles, and bobbins. Also cut the dowels to size. Wind bobbins to save time.

DIRECTIONS

1. Explain the difference between fill-in weaving and complete-line weaving. Fill-in weaving leaves areas to be filled in with other colors or other kinds of fiber.

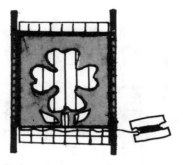

2. The illustration below on the left, shows how the fibers are joined with each other by an interlocking technique. Copy the design on the chalkboard, and demonstrate the method on the unfinished model. The method shown in the illustration on the right, is simpler.

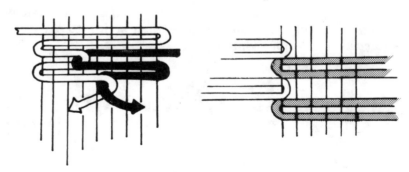

3. Hand out the materials and ask the children to cover their desks.
4. Follow directions 7-10, Activity 47, "Fun with Fiber Weaving." Check all work at this point. Instruct the students to take their dowel sticks and tape them to the sides of the loom.
5. After the looms are strung, tell the students to plan a design on paper that will be simple but recognizable. It will be the size of the strung area of the loom. The shapes should be simple, like that of a fish, a house, a leafy tree, a flower, a face, or a geometric figure. Square off forms where needed. Choose colors to show contrasts. Review work to see that it is kept simple.

6. Now the design can be placed under the warp threads and traced on the threads with a marker. Try to make these outlines in the same color as the shape.

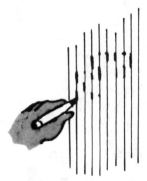

7. Have the students select those fibers that best suit their designs. Tell them to consider texture, color, and value contrasts. Following their design plans, the students will weave the color that will dominate the weaving, such as the background color.
8. Instruct the students to take a second color fiber that will be connecting with the woven color and carefully follow directions. Weave it in the opposite direction, looping next to or through the previous color that is looped around the warp string. Ask the children to refer to the chalkboard plan and the woven model. Continue on with the other colors.
9. Check the weaving progress. Look for mistakes that need correcting before they become difficult to remedy.
10. When the weaving is completed, interesting "extras" like knots, tassels, buttons, beads, etc., may be added.
11. Remove the woven pictures carefully from the loom and take one of the dowel sticks and run it through the top loops. Attach string to the dowel to make the woven picture ready for display.

Activity 49 ═══════════ WEAVING WITH NATURE'S GIFTS (3-6)

This project is especially appealing because the children have control over the materials to be used. They will have the fun of finding the materials outdoors, growing in many places. Grasses, weeds, and leaves can be woven, and found objects such as feathers, seeds, and shells can be attached for added interest.

OBJECTIVES

Art
- Work with subtle natural colors like greens, yellows, and tans.
- Manipulate unusual materials.
- Use a lot of imagination.
- Use cutting, pasting, and assembling skills.

MATERIALS NEEDED

- Covering for desks
- Pencils
- Rulers (for beater)
- Sturdy scissors
- Heavy cardboard (not corrugated) or chipboard
- Sturdy thread
- Mobile wire (optional)
- White glue and applicators
- Colored matboard

- Found materials such as narrow leaves (like willow), grasses (like pampas grass, bamboo grass, silver grass, fragmites grass, blue oat grass, porcupine grass), weeds, palm leaves, corn husks, tassels, etc.
- Found objects such as shells, pebbles, feathers, seeds, etc.

PREPARATION

Gather all the materials collected outdoors. The sizes of these natural materials will determine the size of the looms. Cut out the chipboard looms ahead of time.

DIRECTIONS

1. Hand out the materials and ask the students to cover their desks.
2. Follow directions 7-10, Activity 47, Fun with Fiber Weaving.
3. Before starting the weaving, tell the children it is best to first lay out their grasses, etc. on their desk and plan the design.

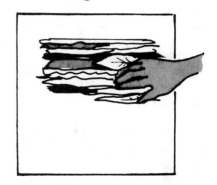

4. Take the beater and weave it under, over, under, over, etc. through the warp threads. Take it and turn it on the side and lift the warp.

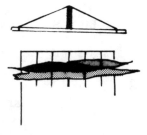

5. Run the grasses and leaves under the raised threads. Repeat the process until the loom is filled. Remove the beater to gently align each woven line.
6. Sew or glue the seeds, shells, feathers, etc., using the thread or mobile wire to attach the objects.
7. Glue the woven construction onto the matboard and put on display.

Activity **50** ══════════════════════ # WHAT TO DO WITH
LEFTOVERS (2-4)

Have your students keep scraps of paper of various colors and shapes cut from previous projects. Challenge the students to take these leftovers and make an imaginative composition. It can be non-objective or it can be made to look like an early American quilt. So, clear out those drawers, and use up those scraps before the year's end!

OBJECTIVES

Art

- ◆ Use previously cut shapes in imaginative ways.
- ◆ Improve cutting and pasting skills.

MATERIALS NEEDED

- Covering for desks
- Scraps of colored construction paper
- White glue and applicators
- Colored construction paper for backing

- Scissors
- Markers
- 12″ × 14″ white construction paper

PREPARATION

Have on hand a good amount of scraps in all sizes, colors, and shapes left over from previous projects, so that the students have plenty of choices for their compositions.

DIRECTIONS

1. Hand out the materials and ask the students to cover their desks and select their scraps.
2. Remind the students to use dark against light for contrast, that scraps can overlap, and that holes can be left to let the background show through. Use design concepts of point, line, and shape. (See Activity 5, 15, and 16.)

3. Challenge the children to use many scrap shapes without extra cutting. Pieces that extend beyond the background can be cut or left as is. Other pieces could have areas that are folded out for dimension.
4. After the pieces are in place, tell the students to carefully glue them in place. Added interest can be made with markers.
5. Place the finished work on display.

FOLLOW-UP

Art

- Make a crazy quilt. Use the same materials as in the above activity. Ask students if there is a quilt in their family that they could show.
- Refer to quilt books for visuals, such as *Twentieth Century Quilts, 1900-1950* by Thomas K. Woodward and Blanche Greenstein (E.P. Dutton).

History
- Present background materials on early American life and how the people kept warm with quilts made from fabric scraps. Not only did they use the quilts on beds, but they were also used in doorways and on windows to keep out the wind and cold.
- Research quilt designs made by Black Americans. Contact The Museum of American Folk Art, 2 Lincoln Square, New York, New York 10019. You can also contact the American Craft Museum, 40 West 53rd Street, New York, New York 10022.

Math

After studying quilt patterns, copy a design based on geometrics. This can help the students make another design of their own creation. A very helpful book is *Patchwork, Applique, and Quilting Primer* by Elyse Sommer (Lothrop, Lee and Shepard Co.).

Activity 51 ══════════════ INSIDE AND OUTSIDE
HALLOWEEN HAPPENINGS (2-4)

Halloween is the time when reality and fantasy can come together. Picture a fun party on Halloween night. Inside, everyone is wearing a costume, drinking soda and cider, eating tasty foods, and playing games. Decorations are all around. Outside, there are flying witches, goblins, bats and black cats. Students will draw a cutaway (like a doll house) lighted interior surrounded by the darkness of the night. The lesson is a study in the contrast of dark and light.

OBJECTIVES

Art
- To work on pencil and painting skills
- To learn about contrast

Language Arts
- To learn to make a short oral presentation

PREPARATION

Draw the basic shapes on the chalkboard.

MATERIALS NEEDED

- 11″ × 17″ black construction paper
- 7″ × 7″ white construction paper
- 12″ × 18″ colored backing paper
- Water
- Tempera paints in white, yellow, purple, green, orange, black
- Pencils and erasers
- Paste and applicators
- Markers and colored pencils
- #2, #7, and #10 brushes

DIRECTIONS

1. Distribute the materials, and ask the students to cover their desks.
2. Tell the students they will be drawing a nighttime Halloween party. The party can be happening at one's home, at a community center, at a recreation center, etc. Or, it could be a fantasy party in a castle, on an airplane, in a spaceship, or in the middle of the earth. Where the party is taking place should be light in color. Outside, the night is dark with blues, greys, purples, and browns. The only light spots would be the moon and its glow.
3. Ask the students to express their feelings about nighttime and why it is different from daytime.
4. Ask the students to begin drawing their scenes in pencil on both the black and white paper. Circulate around and give help where needed.
5. Tell the students that when they are satisfied with their drawings, they can begin painting on the black paper. Remind them that this is a picture of lights and darks. Paint the sky with purples, white, and greys to create a mood. Paint clouds, the moon, bats, etc. The darker the sky, the more easily the party area can be seen. Take the 7″ white square and draw the interior party scene in pencil. Complete with markers and colored pencils. Paste the square on the block paper.
6. When completed, paste the pictures onto the backing paper. Put on display after the oral presentations. These pictures will provide a different kind of Halloween classroom decoration.

FOLLOW-UP

Art

Use the lesson to illustrate other nighttime activities such as those on Christmas Eve, Chanukah, or at birthday parties, scout meetings, etc.

Language Arts

Plan for each student to give a short talk about his or her picture before the class.

Activity 52 ════════════════════ # THE LOTS-OF-LOVE 3-D VALENTINE (5-6)

Making handmade valentines provides the students with the opportunity to express love and appreciation of poetry and decorative, symbolic art. Making a dimensional Victorian-style valentine will challenge their measuring, cutting, folding, and pasting skills. In addition, the students will learn to address envelopes.

OBJECTIVES

Art

* Increase measuring, cutting, pasting, and folding skills.
* Design a greeting card.
* Make an envelope.

Language Arts

* Explore poetry by writing a quatrain.
* Address an envelope.

MATERIALS NEEDED

* Covering for desks
* 8½" × 11" white paper
* 4¼" × 5½" red construction paper
* Pencils
* Erasers

* Colored pencils or markers
* White glue and applicator
* Rulers
* Scissors
* Tape
* 12" × 18" white construction paper for envelopes

PREPARATION

Explain to the students how to compose a four-line poem that will be included in their valentine. It will express love for the person receiving the valentine. Prepare a sample valentine for reference. Also prepare an envelope for students to copy. If envelopes aren't to be made by the students, buy "Baronial No. 5½" envelopes from a stationery store. Ask students to bring in the full names and addresses of those who will receive the valentines, and ask them to bring in stamps. They will learn how to address envelopes.

DIRECTIONS

1. Explain to the students that the valentines they will be making will be similar to those sent in Victorian times (a hundred or so years ago) in this country and England. Show any reference material. Point out that Victorian valentines were three-dimensional and had poetry and a lot of decoration.
2. Hand out the materials and ask the students to cover their desks.
3. Tell the students that they will be learning how to make a French fold by copying you as you demonstrate. Ask them to take the white 8½″ × 11″ paper and align the two shorter sides together to make a fold at the bottom. Turn this bottom fold around so that it is the card's top. Fold the left side over to the right, being careful to get the sides as even as possible. The folded side must be the left side. Check the student's work. Run a ruler along the folds to ensure a nice crisp edge.

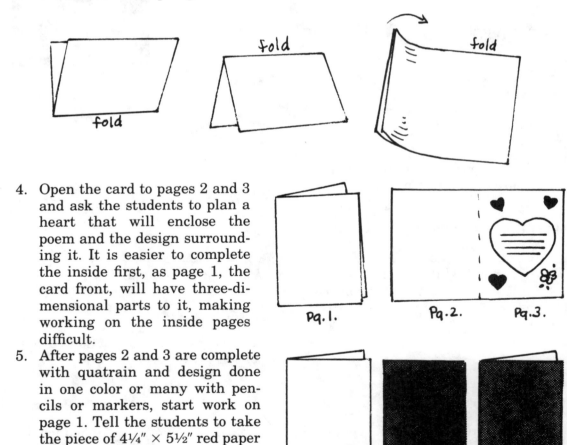

4. Open the card to pages 2 and 3 and ask the students to plan a heart that will enclose the poem and the design surrounding it. It is easier to complete the inside first, as page 1, the card front, will have three-dimensional parts to it, making working on the inside pages difficult.
5. After pages 2 and 3 are complete with quatrain and design done in one color or many with pencils or markers, start work on page 1. Tell the students to take the piece of 4¼″ × 5½″ red paper and paste it to page 1.

174

6. Next, ask the students to take the white paper and measure a 4″ × 5½″ rectangle. Ask them to measure 2″ in from the long sides and make a pencil mark at both top and bottom. Using a ruler lightly connect the marks. Find out if anyone sees that this is the halfway mark. This line will guide them for the heart outline placement. Measure a line at 5″ and another at 5¼″ on the long sides. This will be folded under to make dimension.

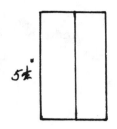

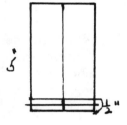

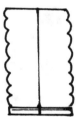

7. Tell the students to take scissors and cut out the rectangle. The scissors can be manipulated in such a way as to create a scalloped or lace-like edge. If students are having difficulty, show how it is done. See that not too much is cut away from the edges. Save leftover white paper for making hinges (explained in step 9).

8. Now tell the students to make the heart shapes for tracing and gluing by folding red paper and cutting them out. Place a heart shape on the rectangle with the heart center following the vertical pencil line. When satisfied with the placement, trace the heart in pencil. This shape will be cut out, allowing the red background to show through. Some help may be needed in cutting out the heart shape.

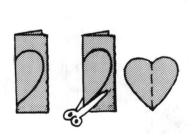

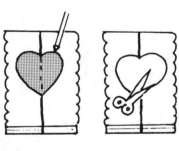

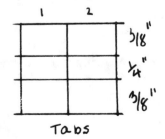

9. For the hinges or tabs, take a piece of scrap white paper and measure two 1″ × ½″ rectangles. Divide these tabs into increments of ⅜″, ¼″, ⅜″. Keep in a safe place so they won't get lost. Cut them out later.

Tabs

10. Go back to the rectangle and draw designs around the cutout heart. Only draw within the 5″ area.

11. When the design is completed, fold under at the two lines. Apply glue to the bottom area and carefully place it on the red paper, leaving about a ¼″ red showing at the bottom. Press the pasted area with the fingers, insuring a good adhesion. A small piece of tape may help with the placement.

12. Cut out the hinges and fold. Apply glue to one of the end areas. Open the heart paper and paste the hinge end to it, beside the cutout heart. Do the same with the other hinge. Apply paste to other hinge ends and carefully place on the red paper surface. Hold in place with thumbs to dry. Looking sideways, the front should have dimension. Now the valentine has the extra look that such dimension brings to it. This part can be adjusted to go into an envelope and pulled in place when removed. Add any lace, ribbon, etc.

13. Making envelopes is rather complicated. First measure the envelope front: 4½″ × 5¾″. Make sure the corners are right angles; avoid making parallelograms. Using a right triangle or checking it against the corner of cardboard or heavy paper can help.

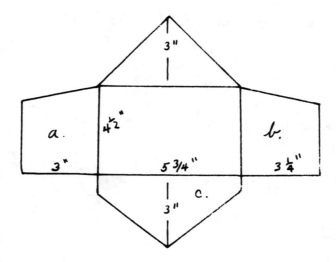

14. After the measurements have been checked, tell the students to carefully cut out the envelope and fold. Fold all flaps toward the center. Tell the students to run their thumbnails or a ruler along the folds to make them sharp.

15. Apply a small amount of white glue to the end of flap "a." Use a small piece of paper or toothpick to paste the envelope. Fold "b" over "a" and hold in place. Be sure not to get any glue on the inside of the envelope. Apply glue to flap "c" and fold it over "a" and "b." Insure a good adhesion by rubbing a fist across the glued areas. It is now ready for addressing, and the valentine will be sent on its way.

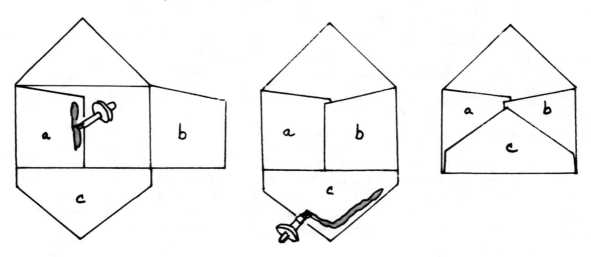

FOLLOW-UP

Art

Dimensional projects on any subject can be constructed by using tabs on cut-out segments and gluing to a background paper or board.

177

Activity **53** ══════════════ **"YOU DRIVE ME BUGGY"**
MASK (K-3)

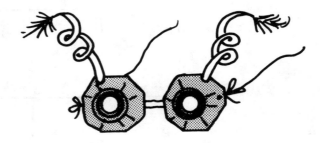

Liven up a flat time-period with this wild bug-mask project made from recyclable materials. Imaginations will take off, and the fun will begin!

OBJECTIVES

Art

- Improve cutting and pasting skills.
- Apply paint on uneven surfaces.
- Use imagination and fact.

Science

- Learn insect construction.
- Become aware of insects' impact on our lives.

MATERIALS NEEDED

- Covering for desks
- Cardboard egg cartons
- Scissors
- White glue and applicators
- Tape
- Straws, wire, or pipe cleaners for antennae
- Tempera paints
- Coffee can lids for palettes
- Brushes
- Water jars
- String for head ties
- Paper punches
- Found objects for decoration

PREPARATION

Collect cardboard egg cartons. Be sure to have extra cartons on hand in case there are any rips or tears that cannot be mended. Either cut the carton ahead of time or mark where the cuts are to be made. Collect plastic coffee can lids for palettes. Try to locate a copy of *Insects: A Golden Nature Guide* or a similar resource such as "Inside the World of the Honeybee" in the August 1959 issue of *National Geographic*.

DIRECTIONS

1. Introduce the lesson by saying to the students, "You're going to drive me buggy—and I'm going to love it!" The activity is a bug-eyed mask made from cardboard egg cartons. Emphasize that bugs (insects) have big compound

eyes for seeing and antennae for feeling their way. The students will be making bug eyes of all colors and antennae into wild and fanciful shapes.

2. Draw a typical insect head on the chalkboard. Draw several body shapes from reference materials.

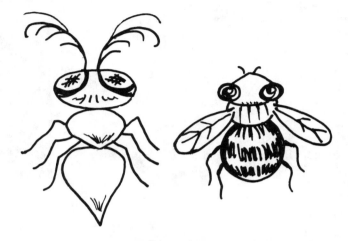

3. Hand out materials and ask students to cover their desks.
4. Instruct the students how to hold the scissors while cutting into the cardboard shapes. They may need help in cutting out the eye holes.
5. When the mask bases are ready, ask the students to begin the painting. Use the plastic coffee can lids for mixing colors.
6. After the paint is dry, stick the antennae into the cardboard. Fasten them from the inside with tape. Be sure no pointed ends are near eyes. Bend and twist into fantastic shapes and decorate with found objects. Use pipe cleaners and tape over nose to hold eyes in place. Again, be careful of eyes. Check all masks.

7. Punch holes and attach string on each side. Tape can be used over the nose. Help tie the masks on the children, and see them drive you buggy!

FOLLOW-UP

Pure Enjoyment
Since all bugs eat a lot, plan a buggy snack party. Ask each "bug" to bring some favorite snacks to this indoor picnic.

Science
* Study "A Day in the Life" of each type of bee.
* Make a list of insects and an accompanying list of their beneficial and/or destructive influence on our lives.

Amaze the class with their own work! By introducing the lower grades to the concept of depth, their outdoor-theme pictures will show a level of maturity without sacrificing the appeal of young students' artwork. This lesson helps strengthen eye and hand coordination.

OBJECTIVES

Art

 ◆ Help build eye-hand coordination.
 ◆ Understand depth (foreground, middle ground, and distance) using color value changes.

MATERIALS NEEDED

- Covering for desks
- Construction paper in all colors
- White chalk
- White glue and applicators
- Rubbing paper
- 9″ × 12″ light blue construction paper

- Dark green, light green, and middle tone green construction paper
- White construction paper for clouds
- 10″ × 13″ dark backing paper
- Colored paper scraps

DIRECTIONS

1. Hand out the materials and ask the students to cover their desks.
2. Tell the students to take their blue paper and lay it on the desks. Draw an irregular line (the horizon line) in white chalk. Then the students will lay the lightest green on it (explain that ground looks lighter in the distance) and draw a similar chalk line on the lightest green.

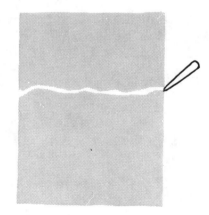

Blue

3. Next, have the students carefully tear along the chalk line on the light green paper.
4. Place this torn paper on the blue background paper. Take the middle tone green paper, and again draw a chalk line and tear.

5. Lay that paper on the light green paper. Draw and tear out the foreground's dark green paper, too.

Greens

6. Take the strips and glue in place on the blue paper.
7. Tell the children that they can add whatever they wish to the picture with more torn paper. Explain that objects look smaller in the distance. Tell them to look out windows and observe. Tear objects out directly without first drawing them. Think of objects such as houses with roofs and chimneys, cars, planes, trees, animals, etc.
8. When completed, mount on backing paper and display.

Activity 55 ================================ PLAN A PUEBLO (1-4)

This is an active learning lesson. Discovering the unique look of the Pueblo Indians' home will inspire the students. Making an adobe village from recyclable cardboard boxes is an exciting challenge. This lesson can also be used as part of Activity 13, Volumes, Part II.

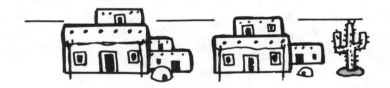

OBJECTIVES

Art
- Work with volumes.
- Make volume size judgments.
- Improve painting skills.
- Use research material effectively.

Geography
- Learn map reading.

Social Studies
- Discover how history connects with life today in the pueblo.

MATERIALS NEEDED

- Cardboard and corrugated boxes of varying sizes (with little or no printed matter)
- Tempera paints
- Coffee can lids for palettes
- Water containers
- Plastic margarine containers for paints
- #4, #6, and #10 paintbrushes
- Stocking "egg" containers (round end) for oven shapes
- Double-face tape
- Liquid dishwashing detergent
- Dropcloths or newspapers to cover floor and/or desks
- White glue
- Paste and applicators
- Paper towels
- Sticks and twigs
- Hemp twine
- Stapler and staples

PREPARATION

Collect boxes of various sizes. Corrugated ones with little or no printing on them are the best. Collect the egg-shaped stocking containers for the oven shapes, and sticks and twigs for ladders, posts, etc. Assemble visual research material of pueblos, such as the February 1964 issue of **National Geographic** for its article "20th Century Indians Preserve Cliff Dwellers' Customs," and the November 1982 issue for "Inside the Sacred Hopi Homeland" (a Pueblo map included). Also check **The Pueblo** by Charlotte and David Yue (New York: Houghton Mifflin, 1986).

DIRECTIONS

1. Show the students all the visuals and ask them what makes these dwellings different from their own homes. Also ask about similarities, such as doors, windows, and steps.
2. Depending on grade level, ask the students to locate the best known pueblos of the United States. The original name of Taos Pueblo is *Red Willow Pueblo;* the Jemez Pueblo, *On the Slope;* and Sandia Pueblo, *Dusty Place.*
3. Hand out the materials, and ask the students to cover their desks or work spaces.
4. Remove any labels and plastic tape from the boxes.
5. Tell the students to arrange the boxes to resemble the pueblo dwellings. Glue and tape in place. Use staples if necessary.

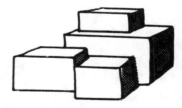

6. Begin mixing the tan adobe color in the plastic bowls. White will be the largest amount of color. Add a smaller amount of yellow and a drop of blue to the white. Set aside some of the color for painting the plastic oven shapes. Mix four parts paint to one part dishwashing liquid. This mixture will adhere to the plastic.

7. Paint the adobe color on the boxes and oven shapes and let dry.
8. When dry, paint in the windows and doors. Refer to photo references. Mix blue and white with a touch of yellow to make turquoise for the window and door trim.
9. Now assemble the pueblo dwellings as shown in the visuals, adding sticks and twigs for beams. Use plasticene for the twig base. Use twine to attach rungs to ladders.

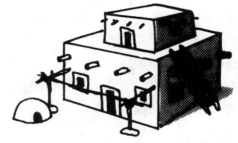

10. To further the realistic look of the setting, you may want to create cacti from recyclable paper towel rolls or from rolled green construction paper. (Directions for making cacti follow.)

MATERIALS NEEDED FOR CACTUS PLANTS

- Covering for desks
- Cardboard paper towel tubes
- Scissors
- Yellow, blue, and white tempera paints or green construction paper
- Coffee can lids for palettes
- Round toothpicks
- Plasticene
- Water containers
- Paper towels
- #2 paintbrushes
- White glue

DIRECTIONS FOR CACTUS PLANTS

1. Cover the desks. Take the tubes or green construction paper and plan shapes similar to the illustration here. Review making cylinders, Activity 12, step 3. Keep cacti size in relation to the pueblo.

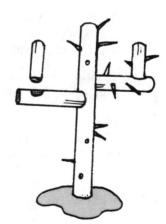

2. Cut and construct the sections to size, and cut holes for the sections to fit together. Construct the cactus. Open ends can be stuffed with paper towels or green paper.
3. Set the cactus in a mound of plasticene.
4. Mix the colors to make the color green desired for tube sections. Paint the cactus and let dry. Then insert toothpick "needles."
5. Put the cacti in place around the pueblo.

FOLLOW-UP

Art

Construct figures as planned in Activity 45, "The First Americans."

Language Arts

Write a report on the history or life today of a pueblo.

Social Studies

Study detailed maps of the pueblo regions.

Geography

Send for "Indian Map of New Mexico," published by Turtle Mountain Publishing Company, 793C Tramway Lane N.E., Albuquerque, New Mexico 87122.

Activity 56 ══════════════ SUMMER SUNSHINE (2-4)

Here is a lesson that challenges the students' painting and writing skills as they look forward to (or recall) a special event during summer vacation or a break.

OBJECTIVES

Art
- Improve watercolor painting skills
- Illustrate a situation from memory.
- Improve outline drawing.
- Improve composition skills.
- Develop self-expression.

Geography
- Develop map reading skills.

Language Arts
- Learn essay writing and short descriptive-sentence writing or list making.
- Read and speak before the class.

PREPARATION

Tell the students ahead of time that they will be making a picture and writing about a summertime event. Ask them to bring in maps that locate where these summer adventures will take (or took) place. Plan time so that this map reading can take place along with essay reading. Work on learning watercolor first, if possible. See Activity 4, Rainbows and Watercolors.

MATERIALS

- Covering for desks
- 8″ × 11″ or 11″ × 17″ heavy white drawing paper or water-color paper
- #4 and #7 watercolor brushes
- Paper towels and tissues
- Pencils and erasers
- Lined paper for writing
- *Permanent* fine-line markers
- Containers of water
- Transparent watercolor sets or tempera paint
- Plastic coffee can tops for palettes
- 9″ × 12″ or 12″ × 18″ colored backing paper
- White glue

DIRECTIONS

1. Review watercolor skills. Demonstrate the use of the brush, moistening of colors, application of watercolor onto paper surface, and flotation of water.
2. Distribute materials, and ask the students to cover their desks.
3. Instruct the students to sketch their composition, showing details of the event that help narrate the story in picture form and that will help in the writing to follow. When corrected and complete, go over the pencil lines with a permanent fine-line marker.
4. When this phase of the lesson is completed, the watercolor is applied. Be careful not to use too much water. Remind the class to work in a free manner, yet to apply the colors where needed within the marker lines. Let color in adjacent areas dry before painting to avoid bleeding.
5. Let completed work dry. Mount on colored background paper with white glue and display. Instruct students to sign their names.
6. Hand out the lined paper for the writing that will describe the activity pictured in the watercolor painting. Lower grades can write a sentence or two or make a list of the important parts of their picture. The upper grades can write a short essay describing the event and how they felt about it. These can be corrected and put on display alongside the pictures.
7. Ask students to read their essays and lists and talk about their pictures.